Dumfries
LIBR
Information
24 HOUR

Pelé

10

First published in 2010

A catalogue record for this book is available from the British Library

ISBN: 978-0-857330-35-2

Published by Haynes Publishing, Sparkford, Yeovil,
Somerset BA22 7JJ, UK
Tel: 01963 442030 Fax: 01963 440001
Int. tel: +44 1963 442030 Int. fax: +44 1963 440001
E-mail: sales@haynes.co.uk
Website: www.haynes.co.uk

Haynes North America Inc., 861 Lawrence Drive,
Newbury Park, California 91320, USA

Creative Director: Kevin Gardner
Designed for Haynes by BrainWave

Printed and bound in the UK

What makes a Great Player from

THE MASTER

10

Contents

10

10 Foreword

Throughout my career I have been repeatedly asked many familiar questions. One of the most common is "what makes a great No.10"? It's a question about which anyone who really loves football has an opinion, but no one has the definitive answer – including me. As a three-time World Cup winner who wore the famous golden No.10 shirt of my country, and as a scorer of over 1,200 goals, I guess I am better placed than most to offer a viewpoint. But I'm unable to give an assured, easy explanation of what makes the No.10 so special.

Some things can't be explained in a few words. To condense the qualities of a world-class attacking footballer simply by saying "he's a great No.10" does not do full justice to their individual talent. The best footballers are not just made, they are born. They have something innate that defines their greatness.

To give you a personal example: when I was a young player during my first professional contract at Baquinho, I noticed that I had an ability to anticipate what was going to happen better than my contemporaries, especially when receiving the ball and being challenged by opponents from behind. Don't get me wrong – my team-mates were very good players, but they didn't have the almost sixth sense that I had. Possessing good peripheral vision helped – it's even been claimed that my eyes are farther apart than most people's, so that I can literally see what's coming a split second before others can – but it's not a matter of physical characteristic. I don't know how, but I just knew what was going to happen on a football field. That's something that can't be taught; no coach can develop such an ability, it's simply something you either have or don't have. It's something special.

In this book, I pay tribute to some of the players who had (or still have) that something special. It's a study of the No.10 position and its most famous practitioners in the modern era from the period around the early 1960s, by which time I

had already won two World Cups. Some I competed against, others I have met or have watched from afar; but all of them have made a lasting impression on me for their goalscoring prowess, their skill, their personality and the way they made the position their own.

Therefore this is a celebration of the No.10's craft and unique appeal. As football fans we may adore goalkeepers, defenders, midfielders and wingers, but it's the central attacking player who remains the one player we can't take our eyes off. He embodies our hopes and expectations, causes us to despair with his failures and near misses, and thrills and excites us with his achievements. No other player carries such responsibility or is the centre of attention to such an exacting degree.

To be a great No.10 requires a mix of different qualities, qualities that can be contradictory. He is a goalscorer, a creator, a target man, a team player but also someone who has to be ruthless and selfish – greedy, even – to fulfill his task. And the differing consequences of what he does can be extreme. The cost of failure can be merciless, in the form of humiliation and outright hate: the potential rewards are both glorious and glamorous. No wonder we are a breed apart!

Each of the No.10s in this book confronted those varied and testing demands at the highest level and succeeded, and all of them at the World Cup. That arena imposed further burdens on their shoulders. Not only were they responsible to their team-mates and management, but also their performances were of vital importance to entire populations – they carried the weight of a nation's expectations. That entails incredible pressure, and only a select few have the temperament and sheer will to meet such a challenge head on and prosper.

Of course, it's not just strength of character that marks out a No.10. It's his intelligence and what he does with his feet and head that make him the best of the best. In this regard, the players selected all boast different attributes. Some were renowned as out-and-out goalscorers, lethal marksmen for

◀ The No.10 surrounded by No.10s. At my soccer school in the US in 1982, I pass on my advice to a crowd of young hopefuls who are dreaming of wearing the famous shirt.

Bidding an emotional farewell to the game against Santos in 1977, I wear the No.10 shirt one last time for New York Cosmos. My great and much missed friend Bobby Moore gives me a hug.

whom goals were just about the only currency of their play. They might not have captured the eye with their all-round contribution or work rate, but their proficiency in achieving the most fundamental aspect of the game – scoring goals – marks them out as superstars.

Others were playmakers that brought out the best in their team-mates, inspiring by example and dominating games. Many could, as the occasion demanded, display admirable bravery as lone target men who selflessly provided for the greater good of the team. Some redefined the central striking role, ranging around the pitch into unexpected positions, bewildering opponents and enrapturing fans. Whatever their particular quality, they wore the No.10 shirt with great distinction and made a lasting impact on the game.

That is not to say that all of them, strictly speaking, are "No.10s". Back in the old days, the number was reserved for central strikers. Now, with the advent of squad numbering systems and the tactical developments that have altered formations, a No.10 may not be the central attacking player. As an example, the winners of the 2006 World Cup featured an attacking midfielder, Francesco Totti, as their No.10, rather than the more conventional front man. Similarly, West Germany's Jürgen Klinsmann, in many ways a No.10 par excellence, wore the No.18 shirt in 1990. So some artistic licence has been adopted in describing a selection of players as "No.10s". The point is that these are the players who fulfilled the role of a No.10, even if they didn't sport the actual number.

Football, as we all know, is about opinions. What follows are some opinions about players, nothing more nor less. No doubt there will be disagreements as to who is featured and some readers will wonder why their particular favourite did not make the cut; but I hope the 20 who are here give a flavour of the No.10 position and illustrate how its most illustrious wearers have played central roles in the seminal moments of the sport's recent history.

For 13 unforgettable years, I was privileged to pull on the No.10 of the Seleção, the same Number I was honoured to wear for Santos. Wearing those shirts conferred on me both great status as well as a duty, but above all gave me joy. I am the author of a much-quoted comment about football being "the beautiful game": I would argue there is nothing more joyful to behold than a No.10 in free flow, scoring goals and playing football the beautiful way.

Pelé

◀ Another shirt I wore with immense pride, that of my club side, Santos.

10

Eusébio

The Predatory Panther

Few strikers were blessed with such power, pace, balance and lethal finishing ability as Eusébio. To see him bursting into the box and unleashing a devastating shot – with either foot – was one of the great sporting spectacles of the 1960s. And he was brave. Though his nickname with the European media was the 'Black Panther', he had the heart of a lion. As an attacker you can't survive at the top level without courage in the face of what will often be brutal defending. Eusébio burst onto the 1966 World Cup with a rush of early goals, but it made him a marked man and he struggled against Nobby Stiles, who was very effective in shackling Eusébio in the semi-final with England. Even so, he finished the tournament as top scorer with nine goals, an outstanding achievement.

One of the all-time greatest goalscorers and ambassadors for the game of football.

Michel Platini

10

◀ Eusébio made quite an impact in the 1966 World Cup in England. Everywhere he went he was mobbed, as here on his departure from Manchester on the team coach after Portugal had beaten Hungary. Like me, he was not afraid to put himself where it hurts, and had a plaster for an eye injury to prove it.

10

Eusébio and I first met on the pitch in the 1962 Intercontinental Cup when Santos played Benfica. After a 3-2 win in the Maracanã in the first leg, we thrashed the Portuguese 5-2 in Lisbon. I scored a hat-trick and I regard it as my finest ever performance, but Eusébio still stood out as a talent to be reckoned with, and scored one of Benfica's consolation goals. We came across each other once more when the two sides met again in 1969. I may have reminded him of the time I managed to slip the ball between his legs in the 1962 game in Lisbon!

◀▲▼
The 1966 World Cup was memorable for Eusébio's prolific and devastating demonstration of the art of goalscoring. He lashed one in against Bulgaria (above), and repeated the trick four times in that outrageous game against North Korea, in which he was sent flying to earn a penalty (left). He scored twice against my own team, Brazil. I could only stand by and admire his performance – literally. I had been injured in the game due to some very rough tackling by Morais and limped my way through to the end, utterly unable to affect the outcome – there were no substitutions in those days. It was not a happy tournament for us, with injuries and management problems contributing to our early exit, but in truth we had no answer to Eusébio. His second goal against us was a real beauty, as he smashed the ball home with a vicious half volley. He raced away to celebrate (left), but, just like us, his own team-mates couldn't catch him that day.

Eusébio never made it to the final. He got as far as the third and fourth place playoff, which must have been a crushing anti-climax having come so close. He did at least play at Wembley, something I regret to say I never managed in my career. After defeat to the hosts in the semi-final he showed what a sporting individual he is by congratulating another gentleman of the game, Bobby Charlton (right).

10

In the playoff with the Soviet Union he scored yet again with a penalty past Lev Yashin. He had some stitches as a souvenir of his time in England, tended to by Portugal's team doctor, João Da Silva Rocha (below). You can't call yourself a genuine No.10 if you don't have a few battle scars.

Player Profile

CAREER STATS

Eusébio

Name: Eusébio da Silva Ferreira

Born: 1942

International Playing Career: 1961–1973

International Appearances: 64

Goals: 41

Clubs: (includes) Sporting Lourenço-Marques, Benfica, Toronto Metros, SC Beira

Did you know...?

Eusébio scored 320 goals in 313 Portuguese league games.

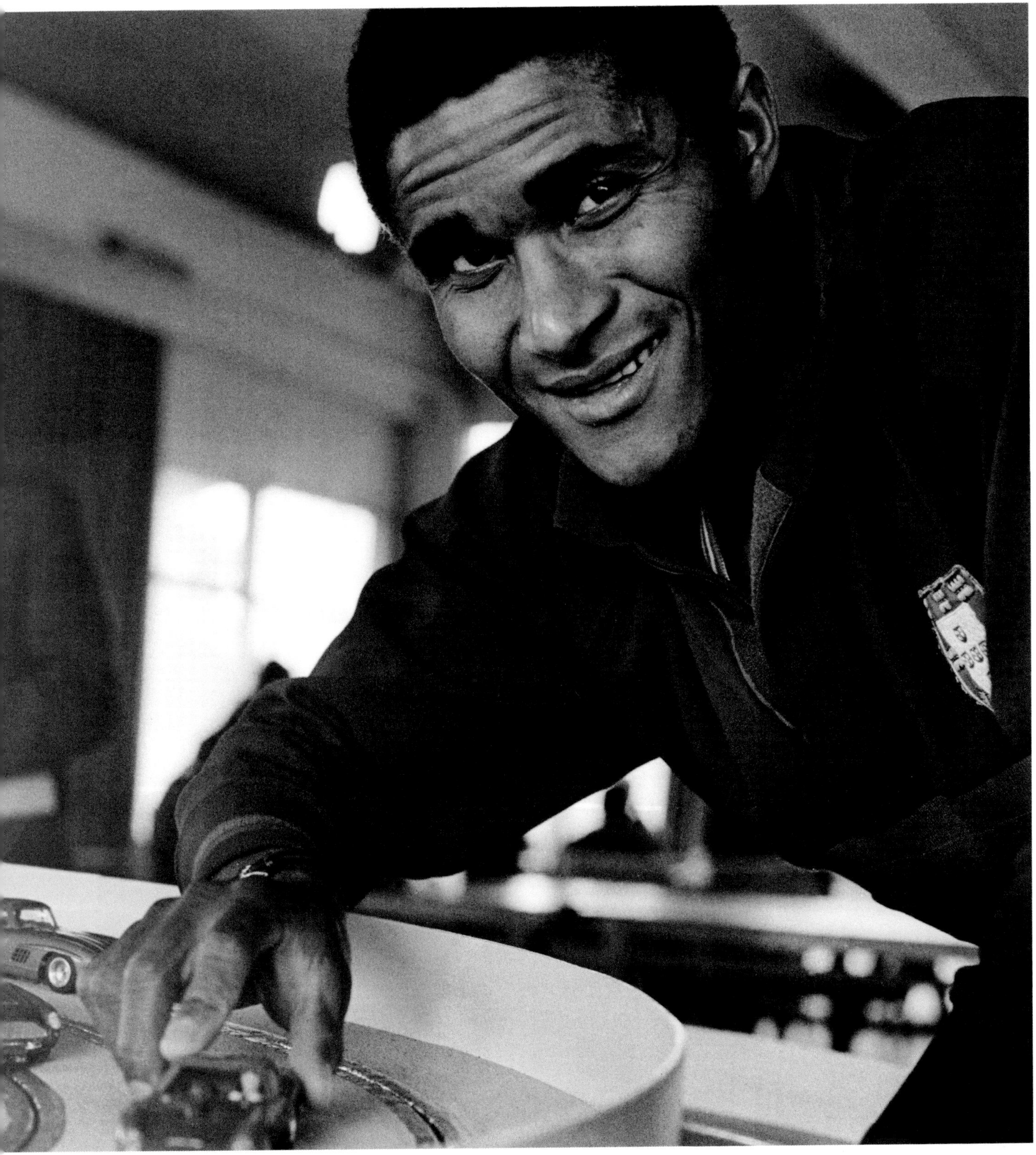

10

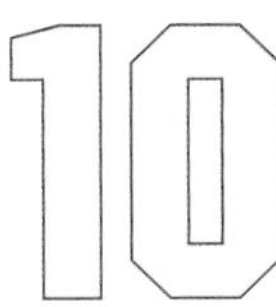

◀
Like many footballers, Eusébio had a taste for fast cars...

10

Eusébio was back in England in 1968 for the European Cup final between Benfica and Manchester United, but again he was on the losing side.

As famous footballers, we've all been recipients of some charming but curious gifts. Eusébio was presented with a football made of ice-cream at a London reception.

Eusébio and I share a taste in good music. I've written quite a few songs myself, and I gather we both have bands named after us.

Physical preparation has always been key. Eusébio was a supremely fit and athletic individual, but the battering he was subjected to took its toll and he finally hung up his boots in 1978 after failing to recover from longstanding knee trouble.

10

Celebrating his 30th birthday with members of his family in January 1972.

◀▲
Few strikers got past the great Gordon Banks, whose famous save against me in the 1970 finals was simply phenomenal. Even in a staged penalty shoot-out with Eusébio, Banks would not be beaten.

10

An image that captures Eusébio in his prime. He terrorized opponents – look how the Hungarian defenders are desperate to keep him at bay.

10

◀ I love this picture. It's a man alone with his thoughts, even under the gaze of admirers at a crowded Manchester airport in 1966. Single-mindedness and focus are key ingredients for any successful No.10 and Eusébio had the ability to use them to his advantage.

10 Müller

Germany's Lethal Weapon

Few strikers have been as ruthless as the great German No.10 Gerd Müller. He may not have had the physique and technical sophistication of an orthodox centre-forward, and he was not the most elegant of players. But appearances can be deceptive. He was a prolific goalscorer, adept at seeing an opportunity and pouncing on any chance with a burst of speed, a quick turn or an impressive show of strength. He starred in two World Cup tournaments. I saw him at close quarters in Mexico in 1970, where he was top scorer with 10 goals. He followed that up with another decisive display four years later in his home country. His goal tally that time was not as great – just four successful strikes – but they were vital nonetheless, particularly the winning goal in the final.

Gerd had his problems after he retired, and as with my compatriot Garrincha, alcohol was at the heart of his difficulties. Thankfully, he's back in the game, and it's wonderful to see him working at his old home, Bayern Munich. The young strikers at the club have no better inspiration than the great Gerd Müller.

In my time, players would stay for years at a club; we played with a little more love. Gerd was at Bayern for 15 years.

10

◀ Müller eludes Holland's Ruud Krol (12) and Arie Haan to score the decisive goal in the 1974 World Cup final.

Müller's predatory instincts proved crucial in the 1974 World Cup game against Poland. West Germany needed just a draw to go through to the final, but the Poles were a good side and the narrow margin of victory reflected a tight contest. Gerd was a marked man, as this shot of him being challenged by Jerzy Gorgon illustrates.

▲
You can't keep a great striker down for long, though. Müller beat Jan Tomaszewski in the 76th minute to seal victory. It was a devastating blow – Müller's nickname "Der Bomber" was so apt because he could destroy sides in an instant.

10

Scoring goals was Müller's business. He notched an amazing 365 at club level in the Bundesliga – an extraordinary figure for such a tough and competitive league. He also thrived in European competition and was a central component of the famous Bayern side, led by Franz Beckenbauer, that won three European Cups in succession between 1974 and 1976.

◀ Gerd was ruled offside in scoring this goal against St Etienne at Hampden Park in the 1976 final.

▼ Back in Scotland and getting his hands on the European Cup once again, with Celtic's famous captain Billy McNeill in 1988.

◀ Müller was a European medal winner as far back as 1967, helping Bayern to beat Glasgow Rangers in Nuremberg.

10 Cruyff

The Total Footballer

My first impression of Johan Cruyff was probably similar to many people's: he didn't really look like a footballer. Of slight build, with his mop of hair, fashionable dress sense and laid-back manner, he seemed to be more like a skinny kid in a rock band than a player who had become a sensation in Holland. But Cruyff was a genius of a footballer and did nothing less than play a significant part in creating a revolutionary new style of football.

He was schooled in the Ajax and Dutch Total Football system; but Cruyff wasn't only a student, he was an innovator. The strategy was based on having players able to switch positions, so a defender could move into attack, a midfielder could drop into defence and so on. Cruyff was just perfect in such a set-up. He was an attacker yet he would range over the whole pitch to such a degree it's hard to describe him in normal terms. One thing I can say with some confidence: the way Cruyff and his Dutch team-mates played they were the deserved inheritors of Brazil's status as the flair team that everyone wanted to watch, even if they couldn't clear the final hurdle and win the World Cup.

10

The free-spirited magician who defied description as a conventional No.10, seen here playing for Ajax in 1972, in his most natural position – with the ball at his feet.

In my opinion you can't get a better illustration of Cruyff's magic than in the opening seconds of the 1974 World Cup final. Holland took the lead through a penalty Cruyff earned before any West German player had touched the ball – and the first one to do so was goalkeeper Sepp Maier, when he picked the ball out of the net! But it's Cruyff's role in the goal that's so remarkable. He first gets possession in his own half – *his own half* – at the start of the move, and when he sets off on his run from the centre circle into the West German box he's the deepest Dutch outfield player. A forward. Incredible. Eventually Berti Vogts (No.2 in the above picture) and Uli Hoeness closed in and he was brought down, which was basically the only way to stop Cruyff in that memorable passage of play.

10

It's a cliché to say such-and-such a player is so gifted that the ball seems stuck to his feet, but it was almost true in Cruyff's case. He was very agile and could flex his body into amazing twists and turns while still keeping his balance and the ball under control. You can see this in the way he rounded Daniel Carnevali to score in a 4-0 win against Argentina.

The other moment that Cruyff will be best remembered for in the 1974 finals was that turn against Sweden. Their full-back Jan Olsson was the one made to look a fool, but his team-mate Inge Ejderstedt was also tied up in knots.

10

Even at a young age, Cruyff served notice to Europe just how good he was. He helped Ajax to an emphatic 7-3 aggregate win over Liverpool in a 1966 European Cup tie at the age of just 19.

Player Profile

CAREER STATS

Johan Cruyff

Name: Hendrick Johan Cruyff
Born: 1947
International Playing Career: 1966–1977
International Appearances: 48
Goals: 33
Clubs: Ajax, Barcelona, Feyenoord, Washington Diplomats, LA Aztecs

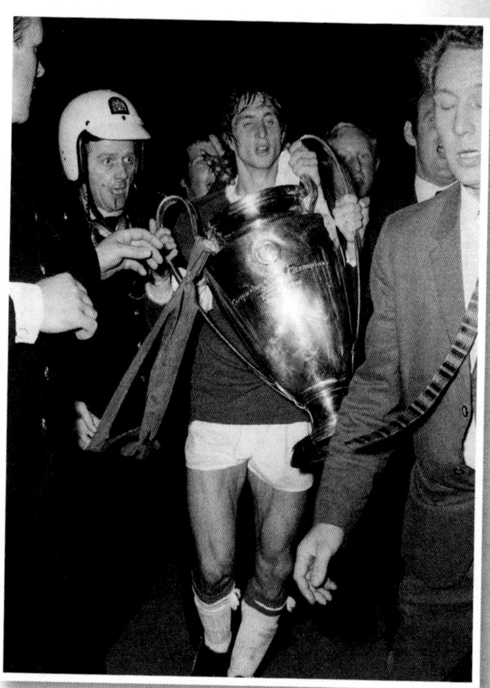

Did you know...?

Due to a separate sponsorship deal, Cruyff had only two black stripes on his Dutch shirt, rather than the three of Holland's kit suppliers, Adidas.

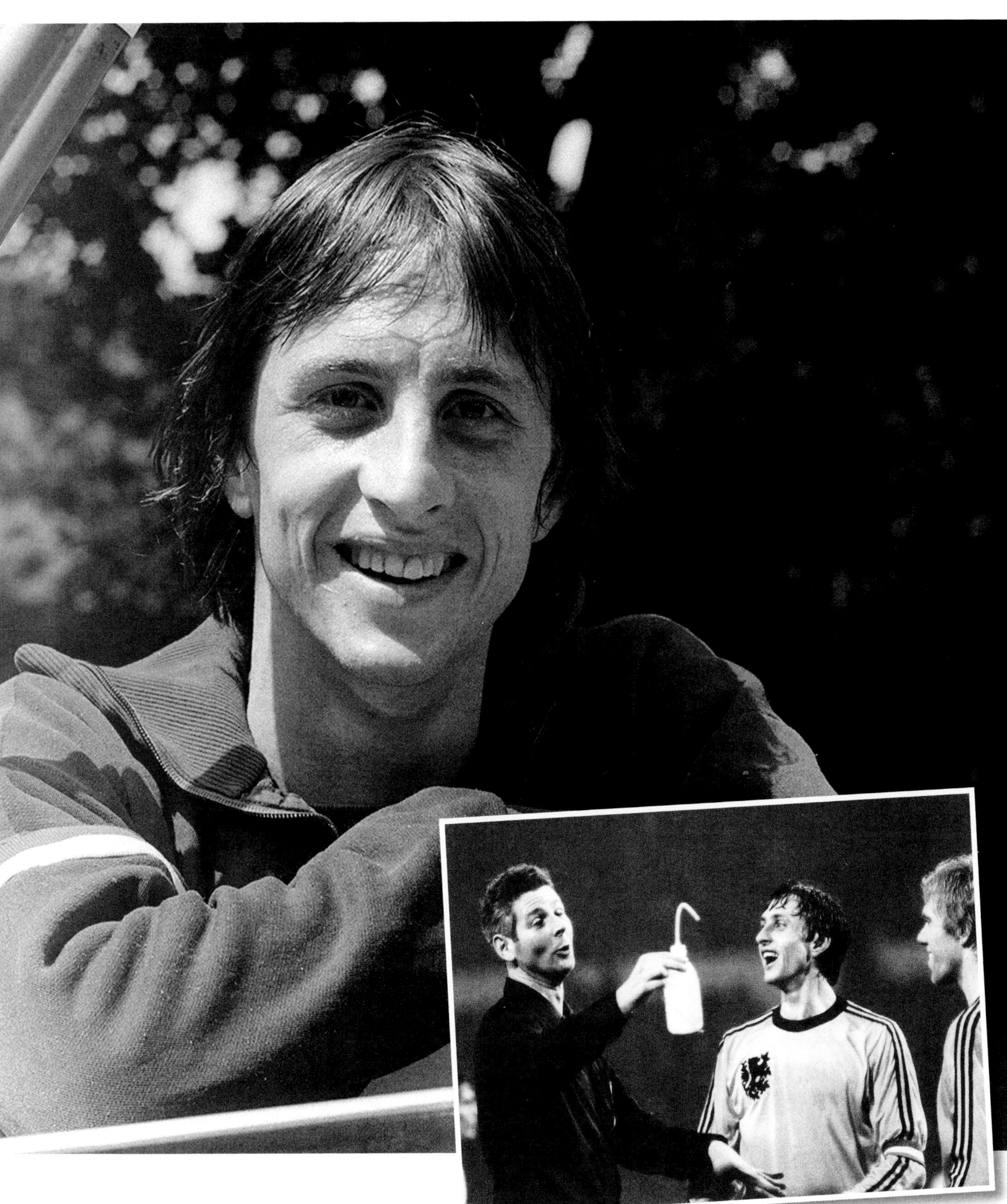

10

Cruyff had a big personality to match his talent, and was a natural with the media. Here he is charming the press before the 1971 European Cup final against Panathanaikos. Cruyff's image certainly helped in gaining attention and he was called the "George Best of Holland". Like many of his countrymen, he wasn't afraid to speak his mind. I respect that in a player – you have to fight your corner.

Sharing a laugh and a joke with the ref during the England v Holland match at Wembley in February 1977.

10

Cruyff transferred to Barcelona in 1973. It was an eventful but largely happy marriage. The club's unique character no doubt appealed to him and his style of play was in the club's best traditions. Cruyff really immersed himself in Catalonian culture and identity, and to this day he's a real hero to their fans. It was at Barca that he scored the famous "phantom goal" when he twisted away from goal but managed to volley home with his back heel.

I never played for a European club side, but headed to North America instead. Cruyff did so too, and spent a season with the LA Aztecs.

The pop star footballer with his superstar car.

For all his image as a bit of a rebel, Johan was a family man at heart. I know the pressures that football can put on the family. Cruyff's was subjected to kidnap threats, but the stability of home life is vital: the older I get the more I realize how important family is.

Cruyff was so at home in Barcelona he gave his son a Catalonian name – Jordi.

10

Part of Cruyff's quality was that he continued to play at a top level well into his 30s. Returning to Holland, he starred for Ajax's arch rivals Feyenoord in a UEFA Cup tie against Tottenham Hotspur in 1983. At 36, he was still pulling the strings.

10

10

Two kindred spirits, two great 'No.10s' – Eusébio and Cruyff.

Ruud Gullit was an admirable successor to Cruyff's position in the Dutch international side.

> "Without the ball you can't win."
>
> *Johan Cruyff*

10

Cruyff went back to Barcelona as coach in 1988. He achieved more as a manager at the Nou Camp then he did as a player, winning four league titles and other trophies, all the while sticking to his football principles. He and I share a philosophy. We may have expressed it in different words (for me it was *jogo bonito* or the "beautiful game") but it means much the same thing: there's a right way to play the game.

10 Henry

Vive la Différence!

Like any great striker he still retains some fundamental qualities: speed, control, touch and outstanding goalscoring ability. But whether in the French national side, with Arsenal or at Barcelona, Henry offers something different. Modern tactics and the improved fitness of players have meant strikers have had to up their game in order to break down defences. Henry can produce the unexpected – a little turn, a burst of speed with the ball under close control, or a killer pass when opponents least expect it. Henry is the complete contemporary No.10 in that he sets up as many goals as he scores.

A No.10 has good control and vision but he has to be special for the team. Henry is a special team player.

10

◀ Thierry Henry is one of a new breed of No.10s. He's adaptable, can be switched around in different formations, and pulls defences apart with his movement.

Henry struggled in Italy with Juventus, but his talent flourished under Arsène Wenger at Arsenal. It was a great move for the player and proved to be just as beneficial to the London club. Wenger was coach at Henry's first club, Monaco, and he knew how to get the best out of him. That kind of relationship can make such a difference, because a manager who believes in you gives you so much confidence and belief. At Arsenal, it took him some time to settle and he didn't score in his first eight games. Thankfully Wenger is patient, and soon Henry was free to express himself, drifting out to the left flank and springing from deep to instigate lightning fast attacks. It was a joy to watch and proved to be massively successful, helping Arsenal towards their remarkable unbeaten league season in 2003/4.

At international level, Henry has won the World Cup and the European Championships and holds the record as top scorer for the French with 51 goals to date. Some of his critics claim he has not produced in the big games, but those kinds of achievements and statistics speak for themselves.

Henry has the physique and body strength that's required to succeed in the modern game. He's had his fair share of knocks but, even when people were writing him off, saying various injuries had ended his time at the top, he's come back and proved them wrong.

10

10

King Thierry... Henry left Arsenal for even greater success at Barcelona, but he remains a legend for the Londoners, and is the club's record goalscorer with 226 goals. For me there are few strikers who compare with him in the modern era because he has produced at top clubs in different leagues and at international level.

10 Puskás

The Magical Major

Ferenc Puskás celebrates the third of his four goals in Real Madrid's famous exhibition of footballing artistry, in which they took Eintracht Frankfurt apart, winning 7-3 in the 1960 European Cup final. I wasn't among the huge crowd in Glasgow's Hampden Park to witness it in person, but, like everyone in football, I was impressed – it had a significant impact on the sport as a whole, influencing a generation of players and managers to come. Madrid were the best club side in the world, and Puskás, the chubby little Hungarian, was among the world's greatest players at the time. He had a left foot to die for, but dominated games with his incisive play like few other No.10s have managed to achieve before or since.

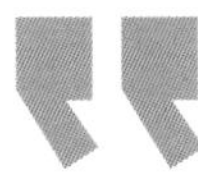

Fantastic players are born.

Pelé

10

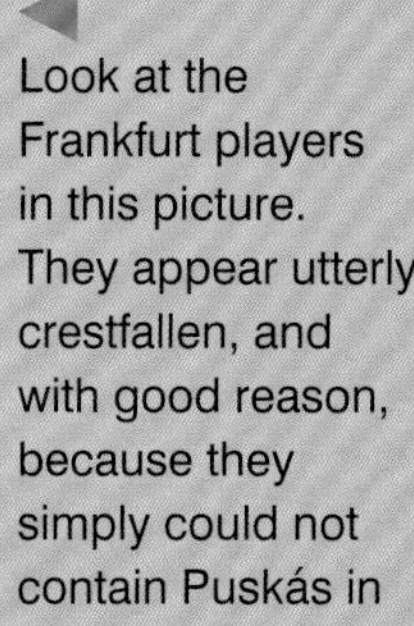

◀ Look at the Frankfurt players in this picture. They appear utterly crestfallen, and with good reason, because they simply could not contain Puskás in that kind of form.

10

Puskás was an inspirational figure and was mobbed ahead of the game against Frankfurt. It's worth remembering that in that day and age there was very little televised football and certainly no computers or video games, so players from other countries were not as familiar to fans as they are today. Having a superstar like Puskás in your midst was a rarity and a real attraction.

Made to feel at home at a Hungarian Sports Exhibition in London in November 1953. Puskás's trip to England that year had been most enjoyable...

10

England goalkeeper Gil Merrick is left helpless by Puskás's powerful drive during Hungary's 6-3 trouncing of the nation that gave football to the world. This was one of those defining games in football history and Puskás, played a central role in the action.

The 'Magical Magyars' were beautiful to watch. Passing and movement, control, imagination, a deft pass here, a neat flick there – they had it all. Puskás provided the most unforgettable moment, dragging the ball back and leaving England's Billy Wright tackling thin air as he scored.

10

His left foot was like a hand. He could do anything with it. In the showers he could even juggle with the soap.

Francisco Gento

Player Profile

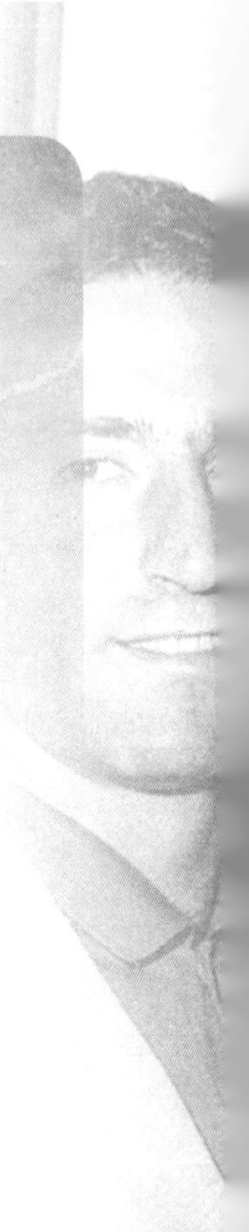

CAREER STATS

Ferenc Puskás

Name: Ferenc Puskás Biro
Born: 1927
Died: 2006
International Playing Career: 1945–1962
International Appearances: 88 (Hungary and Spain)
Goals: 84
Clubs: Honved, Real Madrid

Did you know...?

Puskás played for two national sides after he defected from Hungary in 1956 and emigrated to Spain.

10

With his illustrious Madrid teammates Francisco Gento, José Emilio Santamaria and the great Alfredo di Stefano.

Puskás shows off the European Cup to receptionists at Madrid's team hotel.

Puskás was all smiles, but he had a wily streak as well. When Hungary knocked Brazil out of the 1954 World Cup, there were allegations that Puskás, injured and watching from the sidelines, hit one of our players with a bottle.

10

Hungary dominated football during the first half of the 1950s but missed out on the World Cup, beaten by West Germany in a shock defeat in 1954. By 1966 Puskás was back in London, and ball-juggling in a park – an echo of the way he performed a few tricks in the centre-circle before kick-off in Hungary's 6-3 defeat of England.

10

Puskás took his talent to Greece and Panathanaikos in 1971, coaching them to a European Cup final within a year. He was known as the "Galloping Major", a nickname that stems from his status as an officer at Honved, the Hungarian Army team. He was also called the "Booming Cannon", which I think is more appropriate.

Well, we all get a little out of shape when we retire!

Puskás was reunited with another grand old man of football, Billy Wright, in December 1993. By then Puskás had been allowed back to manage the Hungarian national team.

In his old age, Puskás became an elder statesman of the game, one of a select few whose fame and renown transcends club and national loyalties.

Puskás leads a Rest of the World team that had played England at Wembley in October 1963.

10

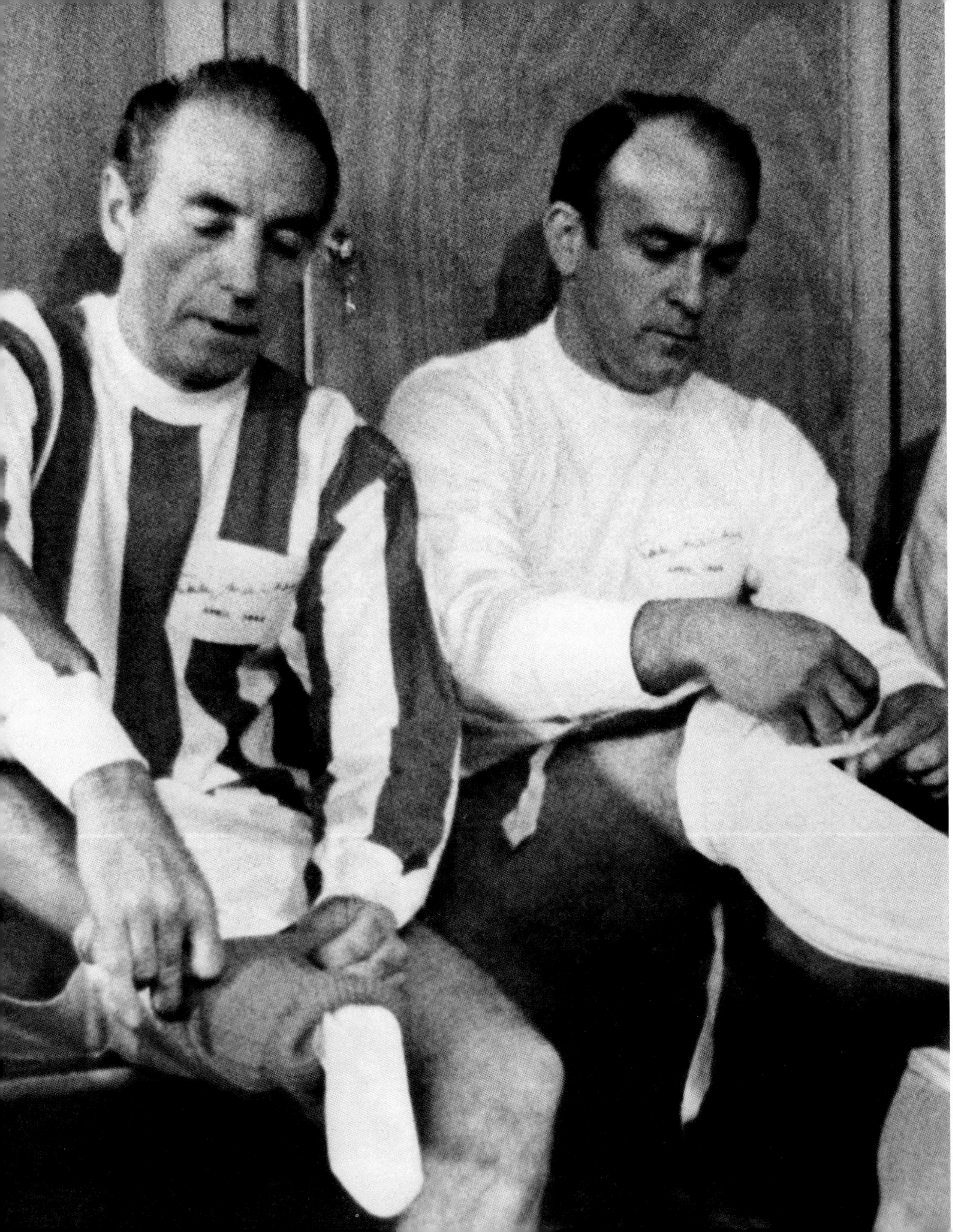

10

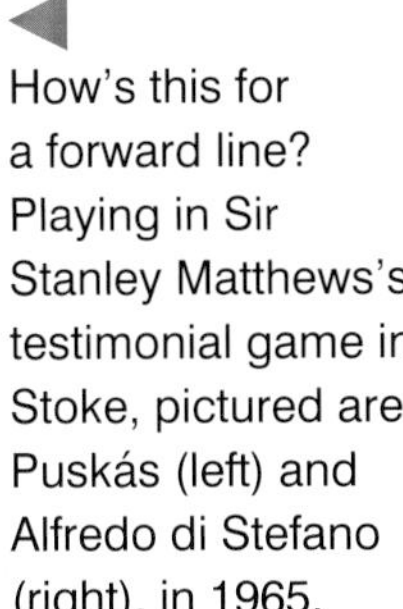

How's this for a forward line? Playing in Sir Stanley Matthews's testimonial game in Stoke, pictured are Puskás (left) and Alfredo di Stefano (right), in 1965.

10 Gullit

The Modern Dutch Master

Ruud Gullit is one of my favourite No.10s from the modern era. Like Thierry Henry, he's another who has both adapted to and influenced how the attacking game is played. Teaming up with fellow Dutchmen Frank Rijkaard and Marco van Basten (one of the best out-and-out goalscorers I have ever seen) at AC Milan, Gullit reigned for a period as the world's best player. For club and country he was a dominating presence, leading the forward line and bringing team-mates into play with his vision and range of passing.

A No.10 who had more physicality and aggression than some of the others, Gullit would always be in my team.

10

Like all good Dutch players, he had excellent technique, but he was also blessed with great balance and impressive physical strength, using his power to fend off even the most determined of defenders.

10

Gullit achieved something no other Dutch captain has – he lifted a trophy. It's a real shame that Holland, for all their great teams, have only one cup to show for their brilliance, but after a series of hard luck stories at the World Cup they fully deserved their 1988 European Championships win. Gullit was an inspiration and opened the scoring in the final against the Soviet Union with a blistering header – a prime example of his awesome ability in the air.

10

Ruud was a hero at AC Milan. Headers, free-kicks, long-range drives, dramatic volleys, runs from deep and neat finishes – you name it, he had every kind of goalscoring weapon you could want in a No.10.

10

Another feature of Gullit's all-round quality is that he has been a success in whatever country he has played, in a number of positions and, in retirement, as a manager and media pundit. After success at home in Holland and magnificent achievements in Italy, he switched to England and thrived as a midfielder at Chelsea. He was one of the first new superstars to come to the English game during the 1990s and was adored by fans (below), won silverware with Chelsea (right), pitted his managerial wits against masters like Sir Alex Ferguson (opposite right), and was an articulate analyst on TV (opposite inset, with Alan Hansen). He was also responsible for one of the more colourful descriptions of the game, saying he was a fan of "sexy football". Not quite the beautiful game, but I know exactly what he meant!

10 Lineker

England's Golden Goalscorer

I recall that Gary Lineker himself once said his speciality was being able to "attack the space", meaning that he would take a gamble, anticipate where a chance might arise and get into position quickly before the defender had time to react. That's a kind of intuitive sense all the best goalscorers have – knowing when and where to make the right move. It requires a very sharp and intelligent football brain to play like this, and a highly tuned understanding of your team-mates. Knowing in advance the kind of pass a colleague will deliver enables a striker to gain a slight advantage that can prove so crucial, and Lineker was a master of the craft.

My dad once said 'Listen, God gave you the gift to play football. But if you're in shape and take care of yourself, no one is going to stop you.

10

◀ England has produced a succession of famous No.10s, and for me Gary Lineker is right up there with the best. A star of two World Cups and a Golden Boot winner, he was a natural goal poacher and lethal in and around the six-yard box, as can be seen in this shot when he scored an opportunistic goal against Poland in the 1986 tournament. Darting towards the near post he arrived that split second before the defender to convert the cross.

10

Lineker first came to global attention with his performances at the 1986 World Cup. Though England were knocked out at the quarter-final stage, and a certain Diego Maradona stole the show, Lineker announced himself as a world class talent, becoming the only Englishman to win the Golden Boot.

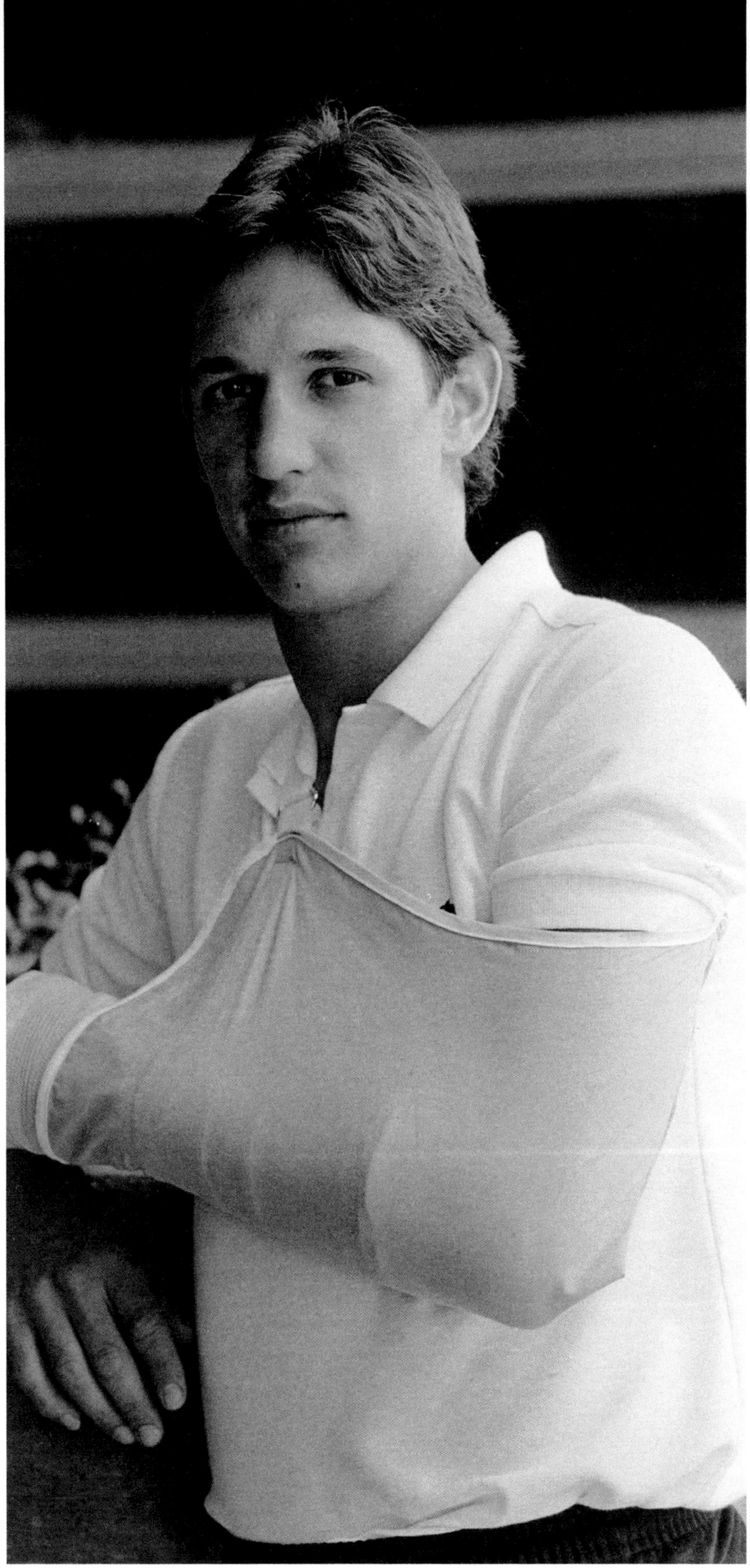

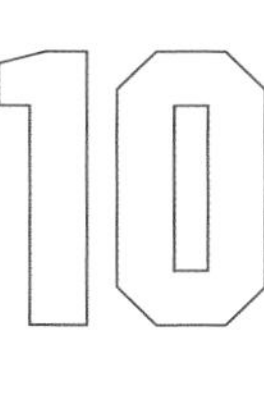

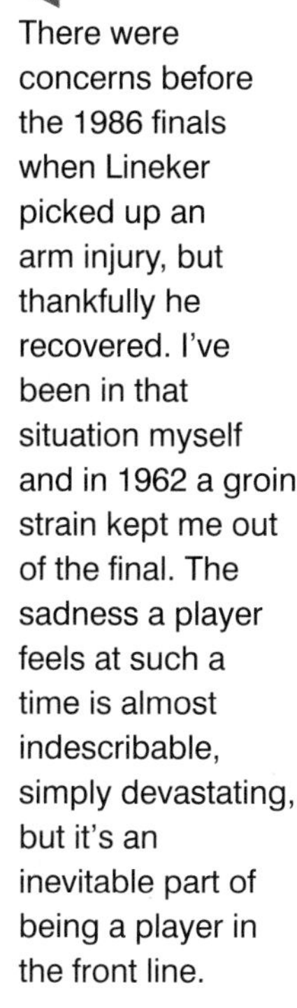

There were concerns before the 1986 finals when Lineker picked up an arm injury, but thankfully he recovered. I've been in that situation myself and in 1962 a groin strain kept me out of the final. The sadness a player feels at such a time is almost indescribable, simply devastating, but it's an inevitable part of being a player in the front line.

Player Profile

CAREER STATS

Gary Lineker

Name: Gary Winston Lineker

Born: 1960

International Playing Career: 1984–1992

International Appearances: 80

Goals: 48

Clubs: Leicester City, Everton, Barcelona, Tottenham Hotspur, Nagoya Grampus Eight

Did you know...?

Lineker was never booked throughout a 16-year playing career.

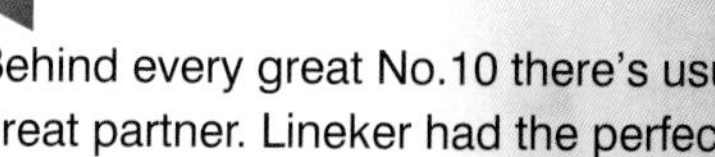

◀ Behind every great No.10 there's usually a great partner. Lineker had the perfect right-hand man in Peter Beardsley.

◀ Lineker scored his sixth goal of the tournament in the quarter-final, but it was not enough to hold off Argentina.

10

In 1990 England and Lineker went even closer, missing out on the final after a nail-biting penalty shoot-out defeat to West Germany. It was the tournament's best game and Lineker again made his mark, scoring an equalizer in normal time (right) and then keeping his cool to strike home in the shoot-out (opposite right). He was Mr Reliable, and 10 goals over two World Cups make him England's most successful striker in the finals.

Football is a simple game: 22 men chase a ball for 90 minutes and, at the end, the Germans always win.

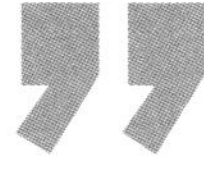

Gary Lineker

Agony for Gary as he misses a penalty against Brazil in a friendly at Wembley. Had he succeeded he would have equalled Bobby Charlton's all-time goalscoring record.

In his final game for his country against Sweden in the 1992 European Championships, Lineker was substituted and with it went his chance of scoring that iconic 49th goal.

When people say of a player that he'd bleed for his country, in Gary Lineker's case it was true. Gary was brave, as well as brilliant.

Lineker as a youngster at Leicester City. Years later, he would return to help save his hometown club from going out of business.

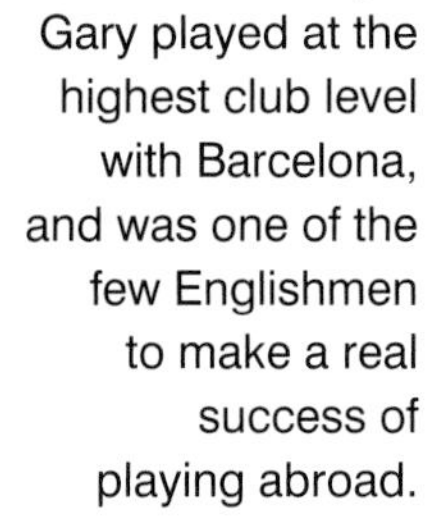

Gary played at the highest club level with Barcelona, and was one of the few Englishmen to make a real success of playing abroad.

10

10

One of the finest players in history presents Gary with his English Footballer of the Year trophy in 1986.

When you're a top footballer, it's also important to conduct yourself in the right way – for your team and your country. I have the highest admiration for people who set an example on the field of play, and Gary Lineker is a true gentleman. He's a fine role model for aspiring young players: play fair, work hard, try your best and you'll deserve any rewards that come your way.

Receiving the Golden Boot from England manager Bobby Robson.

Lineker with his own special award and England's 1990 fairplay award.

Now a respected broadcaster, Gary takes great pride in his ambassadorial and charity work, something close to my heart also. We've both found renewed fulfilment and purpose in life after having hung up our boots.

10 Hurst

Hero for a Day

I'm not sure everyone will agree with the inclusion of Geoff Hurst in the list of legendary No.10s, but he has been selected with good reason. He may not have been the best striker, the most prolific of goalscorers or the most naturally gifted of footballers, but his impact on the game, and one World Cup match in particular, marks him out as a great – *that* game in 1966. Over 40 years on he is still the only man to score a hat-trick in a World Cup final. Here he is pictured with the match ball 30 years later.

Nonetheless, it would be misleading to simply focus on one game, for that would be to ignore Hurst's all-round record and qualities. He played in two World Cups, scored five goals at the finals, hit 24 in total for his country, and won trophies with his club side, West Ham United. Since his retirement he has become a knight of the realm, and a much admired figure in English and world football. That's a tribute to a long and successful career, and his abilities as a No.10.

10

Hurst completes his memorable hat-trick in the 1966 final. Not only was it a stunning achievement to score three goals, but it's evidence of Hurst's excellent stamina. Having played on a draining pitch for two hours, Geoff still had the energy and the courage to finish with real style.

Marauding in attack for West Ham...

...and England.

Raising a glass with his former West Ham and England team-mates Martin Peters and Bobby Moore. The friendship and spirit between this trio played a part in England's success.

Hurst wore the Three Lions shirt with obvious pride.

Geoff auctioned his 1966 shirt in part to raise money for a very worthwhile charity, the *Bobby Moore Imperial Cancer Research Fund*. I gave one of the shirts I wore during the 1970 World Cup final to the Italian defender Roberto Rosato. Over 30 years later, the top, still mud-stained from the Azteca Stadium pitch, came up for auction at Christie's in London and was sold for a record-breaking £157,750. So, you see, it really was a golden shirt.

Geoff with his waxwork dummy. He's aged pretty well!

▲
One man who played a big part in Hurst's career was the Azerbaijani linesman Tofik Bakhramov. The official decided that the ball had crossed the line when Hurst smashed a shot off the underside of bar in the 1966 final. The goal stood and the rest is history.

Geoff travelled to the Baku in 2004 when a statue was unveiled in Bakhramov's honour – a nice gesture. In my time I had plenty of disputes with referees, particularly those who I felt didn't offer me enough protection from tough defenders.

10 Zidane

The Great Galactico

Once in a generation a footballer comes along who stands head and shoulders above his contemporaries. Zinedine Zidane graduated from a class of fine French players to establish himself as the world's best, overcoming all before him at club and international level. Zidane has the medals and awards to prove it: a three-time World Player of the Year, a World Cup and European Championships winner, and a multiple champion with his club teams. But these achievements do only partial justice to his talent. To fully appreciate Zidane, you had to watch him play. He was a phenomenon – a sublime mix of flair, skill, elegance, power, control and grace. He orchestrated the teams he played in, prompting from midfield, encouraging and working with his team-mates while still expressing his own magnificent qualities and carrying an awesome threat as he moved forward. That's a mark of a true great – someone who can be the best as an individual but who also brings out the best in his colleagues.

No.10 is the maestro of the team.

10

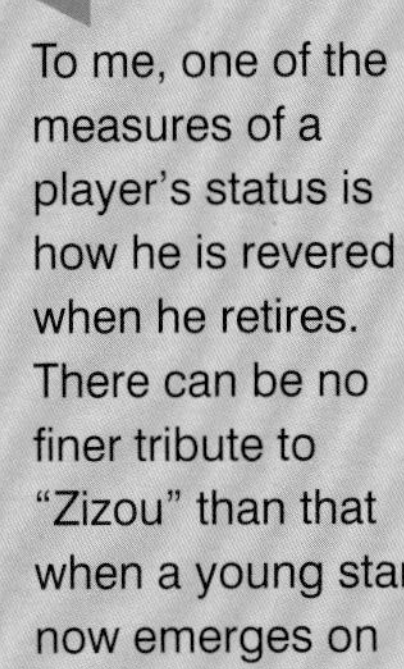

To me, one of the measures of a player's status is how he is revered when he retires. There can be no finer tribute to "Zizou" than that when a young star now emerges on the scene he is described as "the new Zidane".

10

For all the natural talent, Zidane was a real worker. He put in the necessary hours, effort and sweat in training, because without the unglamorous hard graft you haven't got a chance of performing for real on the pitch.

Zidane in action for France, up against one of the best modern English players, Steven Gerrard.

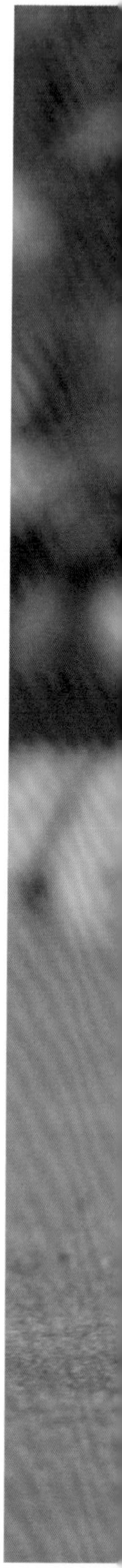

GERRARD
4

Zidane was besieged by fans and the media wherever he went during his career. It comes with the territory; when you are in the public eye, the public want a piece of you.

Zidane was the subject of a film called *Zidane: A 21st Century Portrait*. It was an artistic documentary piece in which the cameras followed him around the pitch during a Real Madrid game: an intriguing concept. I've been involved in a few films, a couple in which I played myself, and one in which I, Bobby Moore, Ossie Ardiles and a few other players got to star alongside Sylvester Stallone and Michael Caine. It's called *Escape to Victory* – a bit of a cult classic. Who knows, there might even be a sequel one day.

10

Europe's Finest

Player Profile

CAREER STATS

Zinedine Zidane

Name: Zinedine Yazid Zidane
Born: 1972
International Playing Career: 1994–2006
International Appearances: 108
Goals: 31
Clubs: Cannes, Bordeaux, Juventus, Real Madrid

Did you know...?

Zidane scored the penalty in "golden goal" extra time that took France to the European Championships final in 2000.

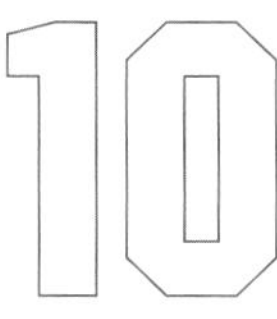

Zidane's success for the French national side was also a symbolic one. Playing in a multiethnic squad alongside the likes of Marcel Desailly, Patrick Vieira, Laurent Blanc and Didier Deschamps, Zidane helped to provide a vivid image of a team – and a country – united.

10

“Sometimes you just want to stop playing just to watch him.”

Christophe Dugarry

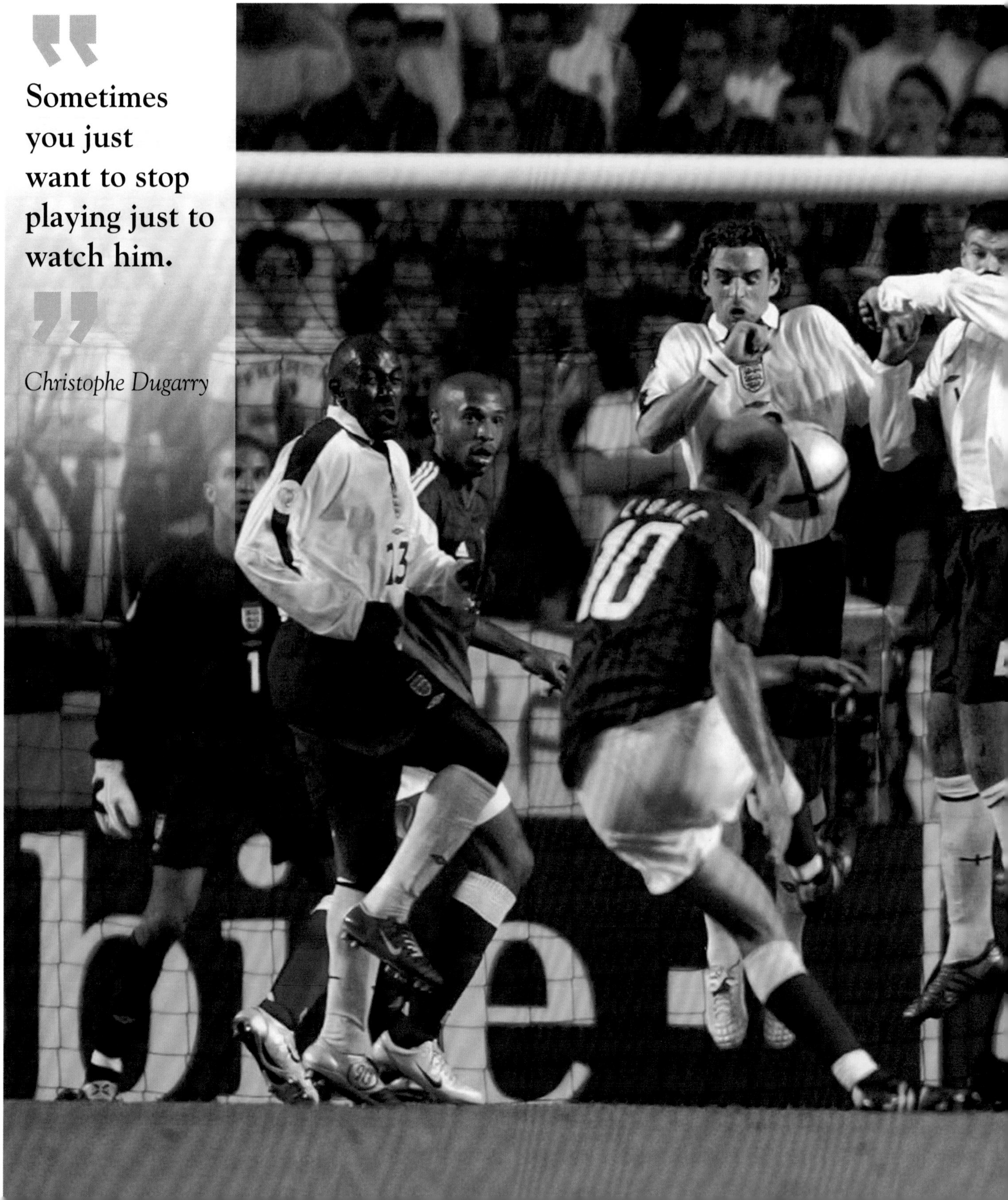

10

Zidane's goal in the 91st minute of the Euro 2004 game against England was one of his best – a beautifully struck and cunningly disguised free-kick that Zidane lifted over and around the wall, confusing goalkeeper David James and curving the ball low into the left-hand side of the net.

10

Arguably Zidane's greatest strike was in the Champions League final of 2002. Perched on the edge of the Bayer Leverkusen penalty area, Zidane waited for a lofted Roberto Carlos cross to come down before thundering it home with his left foot on the volley. It was an extraordinary goal, an ideal illustration of perfect technique and power – and his left foot was supposedly his weakest! It's a strike I never tire of seeing.

10

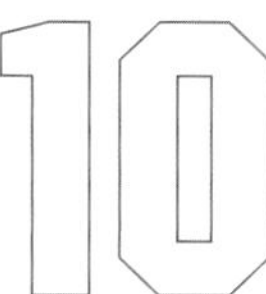

◀ Real Madrid reign victorious, and Zidane is the undisputed king. In a team packed with world-class talent, dubbed “the galacticos”, the Frenchman shone brightest among a star-studded group of players.

10 Garrincha

The Bird of Football Paradise

Of all my Brazilian compatriots who could be included in my selection of the world's best strikers, Garrincha has to top the list. The man known as 'Little Bird' was a genius of a footballer and it was an absolute privilege to play with the man. It's no exaggeration to say that Garrincha is one of the reasons why Brazilian football has been so successful and so adored around the world. He was a captivating figure whose incredible dribbles, dummies, and tricks wowed crowds. Give him the ball and it was virtually impossible for opponents to get it off him. It drove defenders crazy – though it has to be said he could make his team-mates a little mad as well, as we didn't know what he was going to do next, either!

What makes it all the more remarkable that Garrincha made it as a great player was that everything seemed set against him. To take one look at him you would think he was incapable of being a footballer: he was small, had a right leg that bent inwards, and a left leg that was three inches shorter and bent outwards. But it was these physical shortcomings that helped mould him into the superstar he became; he had to struggle to overcome them and this made him terrifically strong and resilient for such a little guy.

A lot has been said and written about this great player's personal life and undeniably he had his fair share of problems. He had an eye for the ladies and the bottle, and it was the latter that proved to be his ultimate weakness, curtailing his life at the woefully young age of 49 – such a tragedy. But his achievements on the pitch with a ball at his mesmerizing feet have ensured him a deserved degree of immortality.

"It's not just about partnerships with other attackers, it's about working with everyone in the team.

10

◀ Garrincha and I at the World Cup in England in 1966. By then we had formed a fantastic partnership – Brazil never lost when we took to the field together. When I was injured during the 1962 World Cup Garrincha was very concerned for my welfare but he was a positive help as well, telling me "you'll get over this and be playing again soon". He even suggested taking me to a faith healer back in his home town of Pau Grande.

10

Garrincha pictured in 1969 with Brazil's 1970 World Cup-winning centre-half, Brito.

Arguably, Garrincha's best performances came in the 1962 World Cup. Though he was, strictly speaking, a right-winger, he's included in this book because he offered so much more in attack than as a straightforward wide man. He scored goals, usually of the spectacular kind, and notched four to share the Golden Boot award, as he displayed his full range of tricks, pace and shooting abilities. He scored a pair of stupendous goals in the defeats of England and Chile. Unfortunately I had to watch from the sidelines due to injury, but to see him in such scintillating form was a joy.

10

It's the 63rd minute of Brazil's meeting with Bulgaria in the 1966 World Cup and Garrincha (No.16) has just unleashed a magnificent curling free-kick with the outside of his right foot that goalkeeper Georgi Naidenov has no hope of keeping out. I'm on the far left of the picture, poised to join in with the celebrations and acclaim my team-mate for his brilliance. What a goal, and what a player.

10

10

Maradona

The Golden Great

Diego Maradona was an unbelievable No.10 – in many people's eyes the best footballer the world has ever seen. Certainly, few players have dominated a tournament like *El pibo d'oro* – "the golden boy" – did in 1986. He inspired his team-mates to victory, almost winning matches on his own with his skill, pace and mesmerizing control. His left foot was one of the sweetest in the game, able to caress delicate passes or propel devastatingly powerful shots. Maradona has never been far from controversy however, and the win over England embodied the beautiful and the bad about this tough little fighter. But when it came to the finer qualities of football, Maradona was a true legend.

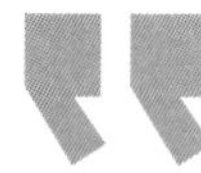

You can have a No.10 who is a completely different player. The person wears the shirt – the shirt doesn't wear the person.

10

1986, the Azteca Stadium and the World Cup quarter-final in Mexico City between England and Argentina. The final whistle has just blown and the greatest player in the world at that time is a picture of unconfined joy as he celebrates a famous victory.

10

Maradona emerged from the Buenos Aires barrios as a superstar in the making, and there was a clamour for him to be picked for the 1978 Argentina World Cup squad. The manager César Luis Menotti resisted and decided to bring him through gradually. By 1980, when he played at Wembley against England, word was spreading about this kid with magic in his boots.

10

The 1982 World Cup wasn't the happiest for Argentina or Maradona, who was sent off in the match against Brazil, but he did show glimpses of his talent, scoring twice against Hungary.

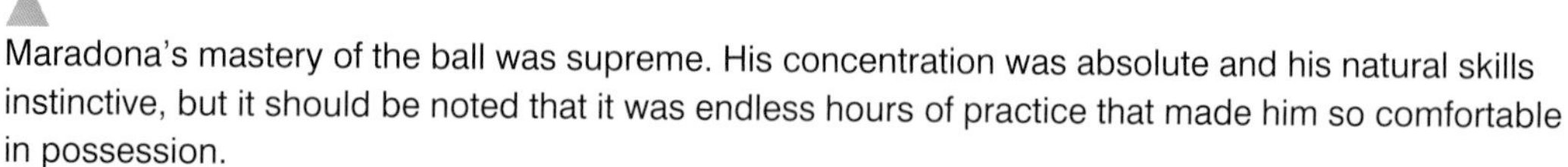

Maradona's mastery of the ball was supreme. His concentration was absolute and his natural skills instinctive, but it should be noted that it was endless hours of practice that made him so comfortable in possession.

In scintillating action against Belgium in 1982. Maradona caused havoc for the Belgians four years later with an almost mirror image of his famous goal against England.

10

Diego was always a competitive and confident player and someone who knew what he wanted on the field.

10

This is how Maradona's career should be remembered. Having scored the controversial "hand of god" goal against England in 1986, he followed it up with one of the finest individual goals the world has ever seen. Springing from his own half he twisted this way and that and eluded almost the entire England team before beating the great Peter Shilton. What a strike!

10

There's an almost comical fuss made about the relationship between Diego Maradona and me. If you believe everything you read and hear you'd think we were constantly at each other's throats. I'm afraid the truth is a little less dramatic. The truth is we have mutual respect for each other's achievements as footballers. Sure, we have our contrasting viewpoints, but that's to be expected: put any two footballers in a room and I guarantee you'll get a difference of opinion on something to do with the game.

The imagined rivalry between us stems in large part from the supposed "anger" we had at sharing the title of FIFA's "Player of the Century". I've got my view, Diego has his, but that doesn't detract from the admiration I have for what he could do on the pitch. I appeared on his TV show *The Night of Number 10* where we shared an honest and good-natured conversation about football, life and lots of things.

The best one-footed player since Puskás.

Sir Stanley Matthews

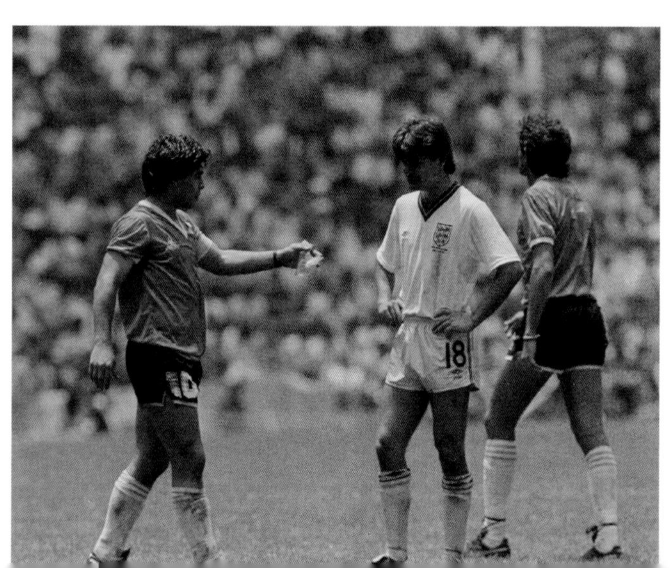

During the Argentina–England game Maradona sportingly handed over some ice to help his opponent Steve Hodge cool down.

Player Profile

CAREER STATS

Diego Maradona

Name: Diego Armando Maradona
Born: 1960
International Playing Career: 1977–1994
International Appearances: 91
Goals: 34
Clubs: Argentinos Juniors, Boca Juniors, Barcelona, Napoli, Sevilla, Newell's Old Boys

Did you know...?

A church has been established in Argentina in Maradona's honour.

10

Maradona played with real passion and commitment.

10

Now Maradona has moved into management, as coach of the national side. That takes some guts. He was always a leader on the pitch but the pressure and expectation of being the manager of your country must be immense.

Everywhere he goes there's always a commotion surrounding Diego.

AFA

10

It's been said of Diego that he's never been more happy as a footballer than when he was on the pitch with a ball at his feet and focusing on the game. That applies to all of us. The other stuff is strictly secondary. In our hearts every No.10 is a lover of the game first and foremost.

10

10

Rivaldo

A Gift for the Spectacular

As I've mentioned before, this book isn't a definitive list of who I think is the absolute best in the position; it's about footballers who have impressed me in the role of attacking player, who have offered something special over a long period or even just a single point in their careers. In Brazil we love players who provide that jaw-dropping moment of skill, an explosive shot, a little move or trick that gets you up off your seat. Vavá, Rivelino, Tostão and Jairzinho were among them; Eder and Socrates of the 1982 team two more, and of the current generation Ronaldinho and Kaká have lived up to a fine tradition.

I believe Rivaldo is a deserving candidate to rank among such company. He was a No.10 who could produce the spectacular and unexpected. Ranging in from the left he was a brilliant dribbler, delivered lightning-quick, precise passes that carved defences open, and he would zip in low shots from all angles. He suffered plenty of deserved criticism for his play-acting in the 2002 World Cup game against Turkey, but that was an indiscretion that should not cloud his achievements – he's a World Cup winner with eight goals in the finals to his enduring credit.

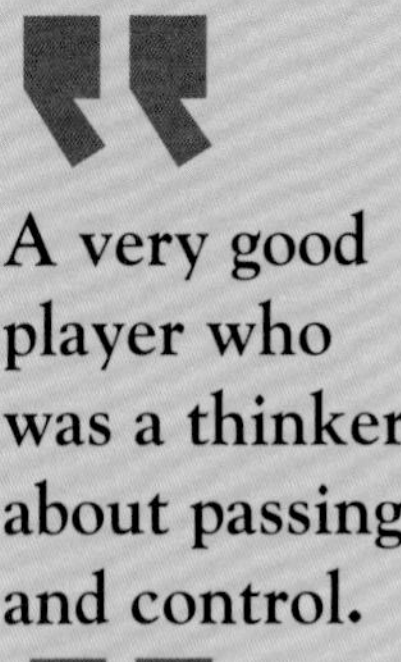

A very good player who was a thinker about passing and control.

10

◀
Choosing Brazilian players for my selection of great No.10s is a very difficult task. There are so many to pick from, and my countrymen have so many different opinions as to who is the best that it's almost impossible to single out one over another without prompting an impassioned debate.

10

▶ Rivaldo in celebratory European action for Barcelona against Leeds United. Perhaps his greatest club performance came in 2001 when Barca needed a win over Valencia to qualify for the Champions League. Rivaldo stepped up with one of *the* great hat-tricks, featuring an amazing last-minute bicycle kick – something I thought was my speciality, though to be fair I didn't score many such goals from *outside* the box!

10

◀ Even a world-class goalkeeper like David Seaman was left helpless in the face of Rivaldo's clinical finishing, as seen here in the 2002 World Cup.

10

▶
One of Rivaldo's specialities was the low, laser-like drive into the corner, despatched with his ever-reliable left foot. Whether for club (right) or country (below), the ruthless effect was much the same.

10

◀
The man with the golden left foot.

10 Charlton

The Football Knight

A star for Manchester United and a World Cup winner with England, Bobby's status in retirement has, if anything, been enhanced and he's become an elder statesman of the game. Knighted for his services to football, he's an ambassador not just for United and England, but for the sport as a whole. Nearly 40 years on since he last pulled on a pair of boots in anger, his qualities as a player are still fresh in my memory. He played with determination and a huge will to win, but also honesty and a respect for his opponents. And what a player he was! A deep-lying forward who would drop into midfield to make penetrating runs on goal before unleashing thunderbolt shots – real net busters! Sir Bobby was, for a good 10 years or so, one of the world's best. To see him in action was a delight; to share a football pitch with him was an honour.

“Modern players don't have the same kind of talent as the young ones from before because they don't play in the street like we used to.”

10

There are very few footballers who are instantly recognized around the world. One such player is Bobby Charlton. From America to Asia, he is famous wherever there are fans of the sport. He's Mr Football, the striker who has come to symbolize all that's good about the English game.

10

Bobby and I were members of that generation of "street" footballers. All over the world, great footballers were brought up in such an environment. Whether it was the terraces of the cold northeast of England where Bobby grew up, or the backstreets of Bauru in Brazil where I used to kick around a ball made of rags, our "schools of soccer" were much the same: close-knit communities, invariably poor, in which working-class kids got the best football education money *couldn't* buy. You learned quick and you learned well. I had my father, a former pro, to thank for being such an influence on my development; Bobby had his mother, Cissie, to teach him how to head the ball.

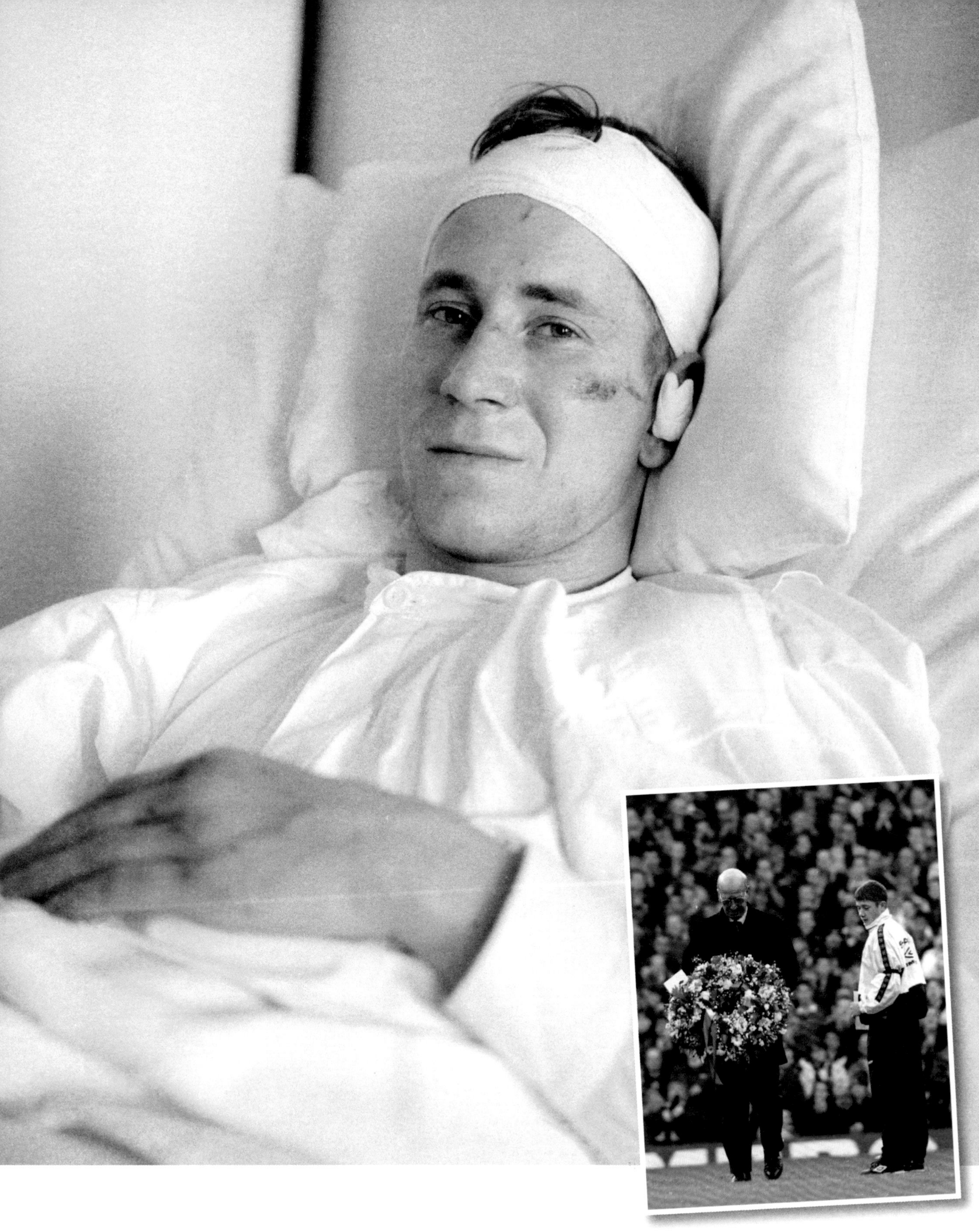

10

Charlton first came to prominence as one of the famous "Busby Babes". That great team had so much promise, but was almost wiped out by the Munich air disaster. Such a tragedy. Bobby suffered relatively light injuries, but to lose so many friends in the disaster must have been just awful. He was back playing within a month and determined to carry on playing in their honour. To recover from such adversity showed great character.

Sir Bobby has never forgotten his friends who died in the crash.

Posing with some models are Law, Best and Charlton: a forward line famous throughout the world. Bobby was the fulcrum of that great trio.

It's a tremendous sadness when a player ends his love affair with his club. Tears poured down my face when I played my final game for Santos, but, nearing 34, I wasn't quite ready to quit for good and laced up my boots once more to play in America. When Bobby called it a day with United in an April 1973 game against Chelsea, he bowed out with typical dignity. His manager and mentor Matt Busby was on hand to pay tribute.

10

◀ Charlton in classic attacking action against Arsenal in 1963. Bobby could strike the ball superbly with either foot.

◀ Perhaps Bobby's finest club hour was when he captained United to victory in the 1968 European Cup final against Benfica. He scored the opening goal in the 4-1 win with a header and finished Benfica off with one of his trademark right-foot scorchers.

Player Profile

CAREER STATS

Bobby Charlton

Name: Sir Robert Charlton
Born: 1937
International Playing Career: 1958–1970
International Appearances: 106
Goals: 49
Clubs: Manchester United, Preston North End

Did you know...?

Charlton is the only player to feature in four World Cup squads for England.

Bobby letting loose with another powerful shot for England.

There are not many footballers worthy of having their portrait displayed in their nation's most prestigious gallery. Charlton gained that honour in 1991, standing proudly beside his friend and England colleague Bobby Moore.

Bobby with his wife, Norma, talking to British Prime Minister Harold Wilson before meeting West German Chancellor, Willy Brandt, at Number 10 Downing Street. Bobby has rubbed shoulders with the great and the good; I also have had the privilege of meeting world leaders, but to become a knight of the British realm must be a tremendous honour.

Charlton was one of the first footballers to be chosen for the British version of *This is Your Life*.

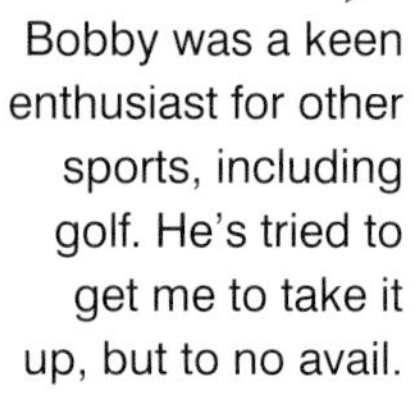

Bobby was a keen enthusiast for other sports, including golf. He's tried to get me to take it up, but to no avail.

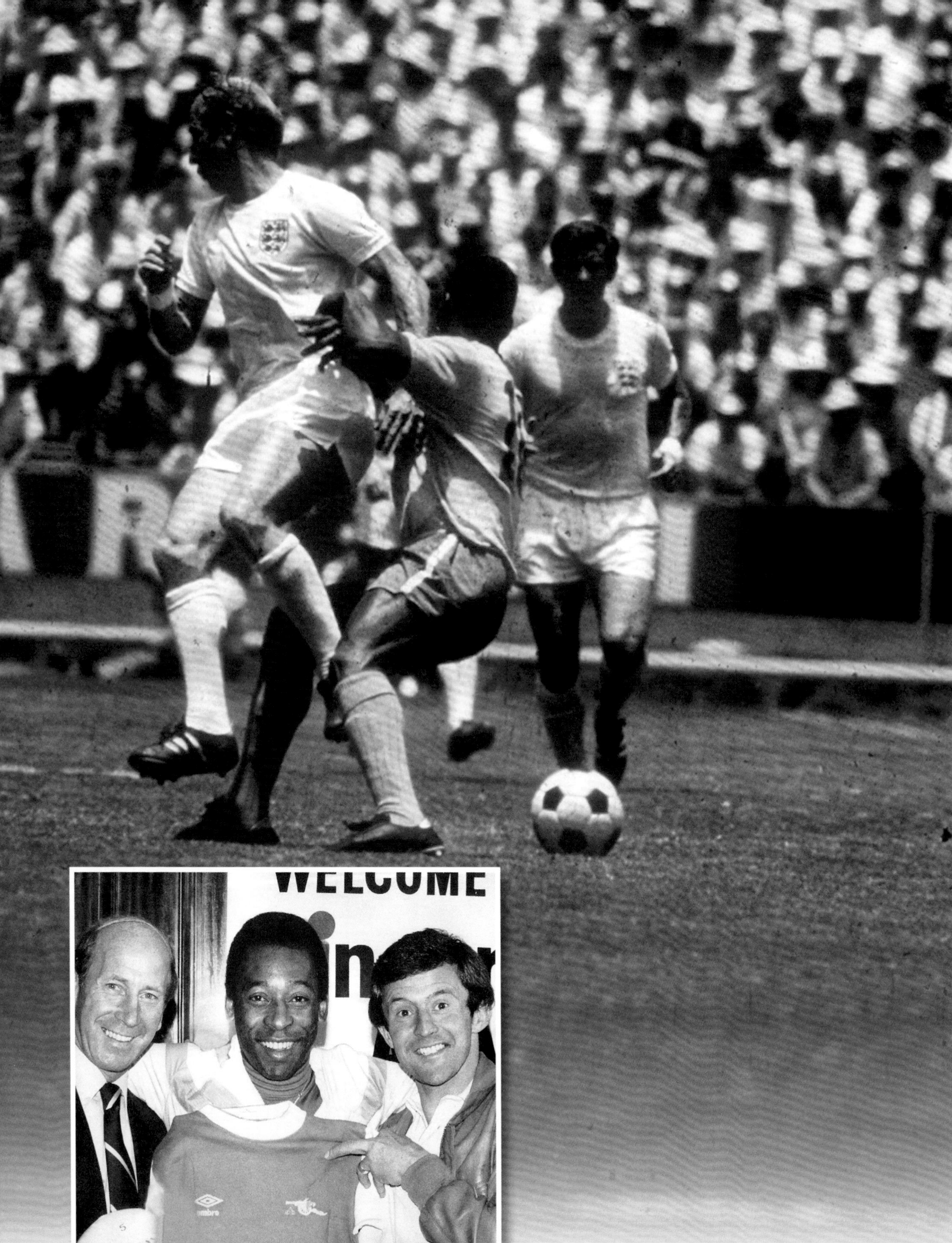

10

Bobby's a good friend. As old adversaries who faced each other in the heat and tension of the Mexico World Cup in 1970 we were competitors, but in retirement we are brothers in arms. We get together when we can, usually meeting when our paths coincide as we travel the world on our various business and charity interests. Here we are (inset) with Arsenal's John Hollins.

10

Bobby in acrobatic action against France during England's victorious 1966 World Cup campaign, the pinnacle of Charlton's career.

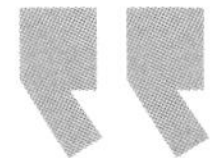

Bobby deserves to keep the record. He was a much better player than me and scored far better goals.

Gary Lineker

Bobby and his brother Jack are united in triumph, a publicly emotional but also touchingly personal moment.

The proud Englishman with 100 of his 106 caps. He still holds the record as England's top goalscorer, with 49. The record will be broken in the end (and I think Wayne Rooney, a tremendous player, will be the one to do it), but Bobby's status is assured.

10

10

What a wonderful picture. Bobby was and still is a football romantic. He won the World Cup, the European Cup, league titles and the FA Cup, but Bobby would enjoy a game anytime, anywhere. You can take the boy out of the street football, but you can't take street football out of the boy.

Bobby has set up a number of soccer schools around the world. Like me he's been keen to pass on his experience and know-how to the next generation of footballers.

10 Rossi

The Penalty Box Predator

For Brazilian fans, the sight of the steely eyed Paolo Rossi might well send shivers down their spines. The Italian striker put paid to the hopes of the nation with a hat-trick that shattered our aim of winning a fourth World Cup in 1982.

It's the mentality that's important.

10

◀
In the 1982 World Cup, Paolo Rossi was a master of the goalscorer's arts. Rossi had taken a while to get going – he didn't get on the scoresheet for the first four games of the campaign – but he timed to perfection his run in to form. It showed that a No.10 doesn't have to dominate the goal charts right from the start, or perform to his utmost throughout a whole tournament. It's about timing: making an impact in the games that matter can be as important a skill for a great striker as knowing when to jump for a header or make a run into space.

10

Rossi gave notice of his talents as a striker in the 1978 World Cup. He scored three goals in Argentina, but such success inevitably made him a marked man.

Training in the foggy gloom in Argentina.

Brazil first encountered Rossi in the third place playoff in 1978. My countrymen were victorious on this occasion, but I suspect this only made Rossi more determined to avenge the defeat the next time our two countries met in earnest.

10

In the 1982 World Cup, Brazil needed only a draw from their final second phase game to qualify for the semi-finals at Italy's expense. Twice Rossi gave his side the lead; twice Brazil drew level. But try as we might to contain Rossi, this lethal penalty box predator had the final say.

▲
He shoots, he scores...

...and he celebrates. Rossi completed his hat-trick in the 74th minute. It sealed a fantastic match, arguably one of the best the World Cup has produced, but that was of little comfort to millions of Brazilians.

►
Rossi celebrates Italy's win over West Germany in the final with team-mate Bruno Conti. In total Rossi scored six goals during the tournament and won the Golden Boot. And to think he might not have made it to Spain in the first place! He had been caught up in a corruption scandal in the Italian league and his international ban was only withdrawn shortly before the tournament began. As I say, it's all about timing.

10 Greaves

Goals, Goals, Goals

Jimmy was not just a goal machine, he was a beautifully composed and elegant footballer who would float across even the muddiest of pitches with the ball under his total mastery. He had a quick-witted intelligence, a shrewd appreciation of what his team-mates could provide for him and what he could reciprocate, and he could read the game like a book.

If goals are the staple diet of a No.10 then Jimmy Greaves feasted as if he was permanently hungry. Wherever he played, whether for club or country, he was outrageously prolific. He scored 410 in total, spread over a 14-year senior professional career. Six times he was top scorer in the English first division; he scored 44 goals in 57 England games, a phenomenal ratio; he scored hat-tricks, poacher's taps-ins, long-range strikes and fantastic individual efforts stemming from mazy runs that carved through hapless defences; his finishing skills were unerringly precise.

When you have the ball the No.10 becomes more important, a leader.

10

◀ I first encountered Jimmy in the 1962 World Cup. Garrincha was on fire and took England apart in our quarter-final meeting, but you could see they had the making of a really good side, and Jimmy stood out as the one to watch. Sadly, injury ruled him out of the final in 1966 and his international career ended a year later, but he still ranks as one of the greatest strikers in the history of the game.

◀▼
Greaves was one of the few Englishmen to try his luck abroad, when he moved to AC Milan in 1961. There were smiles on his arrival at the airport (left) but his heart had never been truly in the switch and it was a short-lived and unsuccessful venture. He lasted barely half a season and found the exacting regime of Milan trainer Nero Rocco and the negative, defensive tactics of Italian football not to his liking. What made things worse was that his life away outside football was pretty miserable. Greaves was kept under virtual lock and key by the club and, when he did manage to get away, his every move was subject to suffocating attention. As a consequence his mood suffered and his form slumped. It's a good illustration of how a player has to be in a good frame of mind to perform.

For all his troubles in Italy, Jimmy was popular with the Milan fans and scored nine goals in 14 appearances, a terrific return made all the more remarkable given the unhappy circumstances. However, no sooner had he packed his family's belongings for leaving England (below) than he was back in the UK.

10

◀ Greaves tried on some sunglasses at the airport before departing for Chile and the 1962 World Cup with team-mate Jimmy Armfield. He grabbed the headlines not just for his fine performances but also for an incident in the game against us, when he caught a stray dog that had somehow found its way onto the pitch. The dog promptly urinated all over him! Garrincha found this so funny that he adopted the animal as a pet.

Greaves was one of those players who played with a smile on his face. For him, football was a game to be enjoyed and to be entertaining for the spectators – a man after my own heart. That's not to say that Jimmy could not be serious; when it came to the importance of winning games, he was a fierce competitor. But as these pictures show, he loved to have a laugh about the game. He was a typical Londoner, a "chirpy cockney" willing to enjoy a joke with his team-mates, other players and referees. Once he even performed a quick dance with our mutual friend Bobby Moore on the pitch during a match!

◀ Playing football with an MP in the mother of all parliaments, the House of Commons.

▼ When he retired Jimmy moved into TV as a pundit and struck up a good double act with the former Liverpool striker Ian St John.

▲ Jimmy and his family in the early years of his retirement. He's had difficulties in his life with alcohol issues, but has shown great strength of character in overcoming the problem and has deservedly become a popular figure in England.

◀ Jimmy hangs out with movie superstar Sean Connery.

10

The great pity for England is that Greaves did not wear the Three Lions shirt more often. His record ranks among the best and he scored more hat-tricks for England than any other player (six). I'm not sure why he didn't play more games during his peak years of the mid- to late 1960s but it's a frustrating "what if" to think what he might have achieved with a greater number of games under his belt. It's worth noting that statistic again, though: 44 goals in 57 matches, a superb strike rate of over 70%. I wonder what he could have achieved with 100 caps?

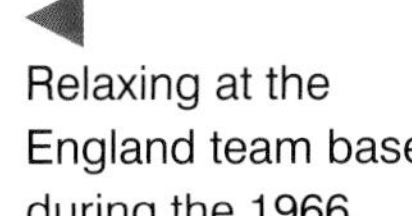

Relaxing at the England team base during the 1966 World Cup.

Greaves came in to the 1966 tournament with high hopes and great expectations. In the opening game against Uruguay, the South Americans knew full well he was the man they had to stop.

10

Greaves was injured in the group game against France in 1966 and with it his World Cup was effectively over. Geoff Hurst came into the side, played well and of course scored that incredible hat-trick in the final. It could have been Jimmy. Instead, he had to sit it out and watch his team-mates achieve immortality. I know how he felt, having suffered a similar experience four years before, but at least I had already won a World Cup medal and had the opportunity for further glory in 1970. Thankfully, Jimmy was finally awarded a winner's medal in 2009 along with the rest of the England squad that didn't play on that day in 1966.

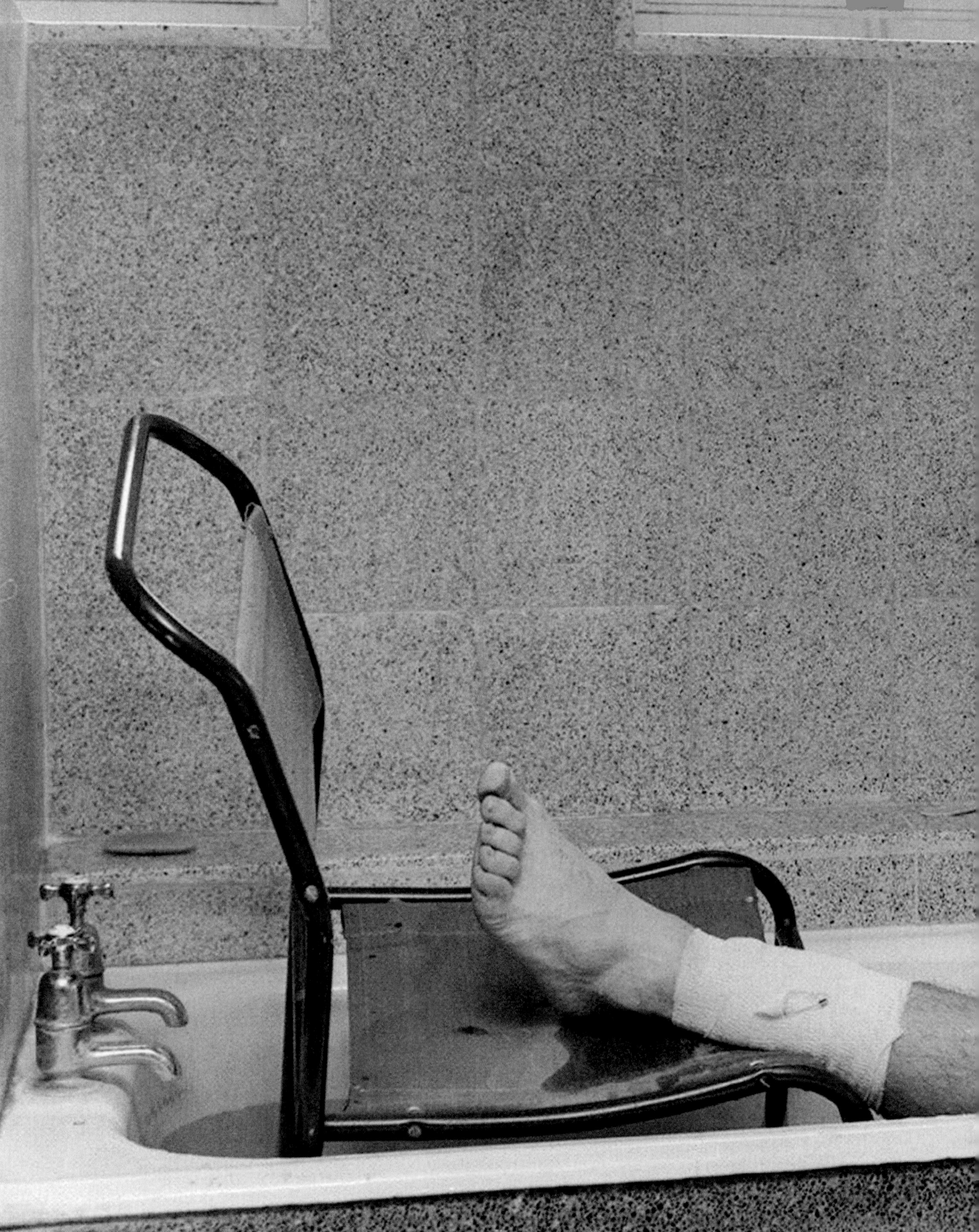

10

He would pass the ball into the net.

Bill Nicholson

Celebrating a 1967 FA Cup semi-final win over Nottingham Forest.

▶▶

Greaves helped Spurs become the first English side to win a European trophy as they won the 1963 Cup Winners' Cup.

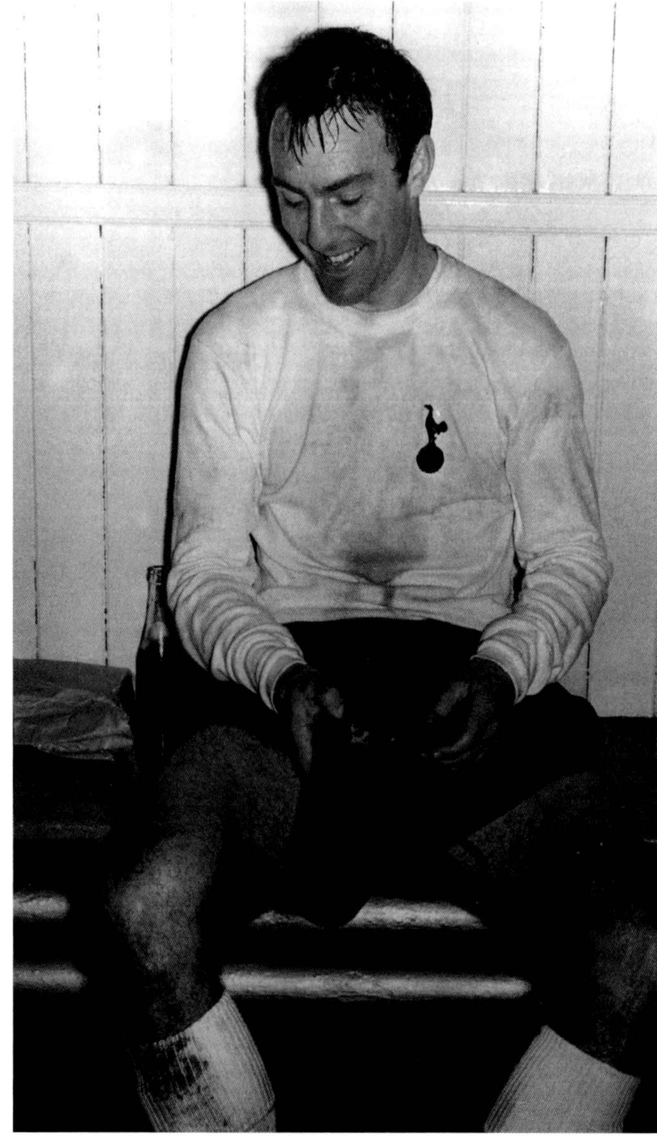

Player Profile

CAREER STATS

Jimmy Greaves

Name: James Peter Greaves
Born: 1940
International Playing Career: 1959–1967
International Appearances: 57
Goals: 44
Clubs: Chelsea, AC Milan, Tottenham Hotspur, West Ham United

Did you know...?

Greaves was the youngest player to score 100 English league goals, hitting that milestone by the age of just 20; he then scored 200 career league goals by the time he was 23.

10

Jimmy scored on his debut for Chelsea, and so began a habit of making an immediate scoring impression in his first game for virtually any subsequent side. On his farewell to Stamford Bridge (left inset) he scored four times.

Greaves's greatest moments came with Tottenham Hotspur (below inset). He joined them the season after they had famously won the league and cup double, and player and team were an ideal match. Here's Jimmy smashing the ball home in a titanic game against Benfica in the European Cup.

10

Coursing through an opposing defence and leaving them trailing: this is how I like to remember Jimmy as a player. Look at his balance and poise. His movement is so graceful, the Mexican defenders look leaden-footed and awkward by comparison.

10

10 Kempes

El Matador

Over nearly 10 years with the Argentina national side spanning three World Cups, and in a club career that ranged from South America to Europe and back again, Kempes scored a total of 311 career goals. He wasn't just a terrific marksman, though, nor solely a penalty-area predator. Athletic and strong, he could come off the defender to drop deep and make penetrating runs into the box. Blessed with an exquisite touch that all Argentinean strikers seem to have, he was an excellent team player as well – in short, he was the ideal No.10.

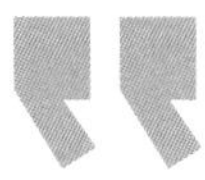

Football can bring people together.

10

Leaping high to celebrate his second and decisive goal in the 1978 World Cup final, Mario Kempes had in the process elevated himself to a position among the great No.10s in the game. Affectionately known as *El Matador*, or “the Killer” in Spain, where he was playing his club football with Valencia, the nickname was appropriate. Kempes was a lethal goalscorer and had the priceless, match-winning ability to punish opposing teams and hurt them where it counts.

10

Kempes returned to Spain for the 1982 World Cup. This time he was wearing the No.11 shirt for Argentina. His reign as the national side's No.10 had ended when Diego Maradona took over the honour. I guess if you are going to make way for anyone, it might as well be one the best players of all time. Mario and Diego's old team-mate Osvaldo Ardiles, a shrewd judge of players, rates Kempes second only to Maradona in the Argentinean hall of fame, which is high praise indeed.

Kempes played his club football in Argentina, Spain and Austria. For a brief moment it looked as if he might be following in the path of his compatriots Ardiles and Ricardo Villa by playing in England for Tottenham Hotspur, and he played in a pre-season trial game in the unlikely surroundings of non-league Enfield Town in 1984. Not quite the Estadio Monumental in 1978, though, and certainly no spectacular ticker-tape reception!

Who says No.10s are only interested in the headline-grabbing glory? Kempes was one striker who would put in the necessary effort and hard work for the team, and did his share of tackling in the 1978 final against Holland. Kempes was the only foreign-based player in the Argentina team, the exception to manager César Luis Menotti's "home" players-only rule. That he was prepared to break his own strictures speaks volumes for how highly Menotti rated the forward.

10

10

Kempes with Leopoldo Luque and Daniel Bertoni, together in victory. Kempes was top scorer in 1978 with six goals, but wasn't the type to monopolize the limelight, saying "it wasn't my goals, or even the final itself, that I'll always remember, but the joy on people's faces". A modest reaction from a great No.10.

10

Zico

The Heir Apparent

I named Zico in my list of the greatest 125 living players and with good reason. Arthur Antunes Coimbra, or Zico as he is better known, is perhaps the player who had most deserving claim to the description "the new Pelé". I don't mean to appear immodest, but it's a fact that every decent attacking player who has emerged in my country has been hailed (and hyped) as my direct successor. That's an unfair burden to place on a man's shoulders, but Zico carried it better than most, and also stands proud as a great player in his own right.

Strictly speaking we played in different positions – Zico is more often regarded as an attacking midfielder than a forward. But Zico and I have shared a philosophy in how we like to see the game played. As a manager who has worked in a number of domestic leagues, Zico is a purist who places fundamental faith in attacking football full of good passing and movement. He had the same mentality as a player, and was a delight to watch. He was a natural on the ball, brilliant at free-kicks and in despatching swerving shots from long range. He was able to turn on the head of a pin and release an inch-perfect pass, an example of how he combined individual excellence with deadly and effective contributions to the benefit of the team.

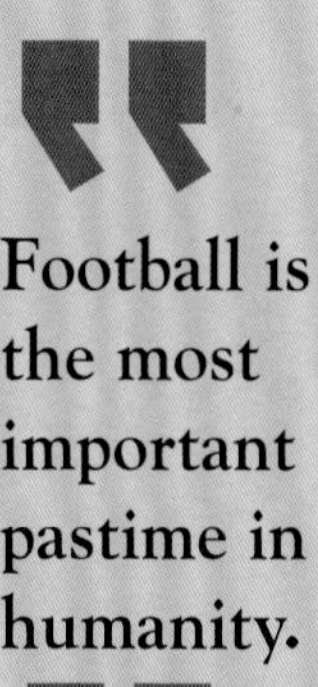

Football is the most important pastime in humanity.

10

◀
A huge success at his beloved Flamengo, Zico was a fluent, flamboyant and dashing attacking player, adored by fans of club and country. Though he missed out on World Cup glory and will for ever be identified as one of the great but ultimately "almost men" of the 1982 *Seleção*, Zico belongs in the ranks of Brazil's finest.

The first player to inherit my No.10 Brazil shirt in the World Cup was Rivelino (above right). He was one of the best players I shared a pitch with and carried the shirt with distinction through to the 1978 tournament, but Zico (above left) was the man in waiting.

10

◀ Zico was treated like a god at the Maracanã Stadium in Rio. He's still the all-time top scorer at the Brazilian football's holiest of holies, with an incredible 333 goals in 435 games.

10

By 1978, Zico (inset) was making a considerable name for himself around the globe. He came over to England for a friendly as a warm up for the World Cup in Argentina and the press there were starting to treat him as the next big thing to emerge from my country. He was inevitably being compared with me, to the extent that some were describing him as the "White Pelé".

◀▲
Zico in action for Brazil against Sweden in 1978 during their First Round Group 3 match in Mar Del Plata. The match was famous, or should I say infamous, for an extraordinary incident in injury time. Nelinho swung over a corner for Zico to head home the winner – but referee Clive Thomas had blown for full time with the ball in flight before Zico scored (left).

Player Profile

CAREER STATS

Zico

Name: Arthur Antunes Coimbra
Born: 1953
International Playing Career: 1976–1988
International Appearances: 72
Goals: 52
Clubs: Flamengo, Udinese, Kashima Antlers

Did you know...?

Zico was part of the Flamengo side that beat Liverpool in the 1981 Intercontinental Club, the first Brazilian side to win the competition since my Santos team in 1963.

Heading down the tunnel after victory over the Soviet Union in the 1982 World Cup.

“I watched the marvellous things he did. When I was a kid, I wanted to be Zico.”

Alex, current Brazilian international

10

◀ Zico sprints past England's Trevor Brooking. They were competing in the American Bicentenary Tournament match in Los Angeles, USA, in 1976.

▲ The 1982 World Cup and (left to right) Falcão, Zico and Eder line up before the Brazil vs. Italy game that decided the fates of both countries. Add in players like Socrates, Junior and Cerezo and it seemed no one could stop us. Unfortunately, Italy had other ideas and exposed the fatal flaw in the team: while Brazil were almost unstoppable going forward, we were vulnerable at the back, and Paolo Rossi punished us in brutal fashion.

◀ The side coached by Tele Santana might not have claimed football's ultimate side but they were fantastic to watch.

▼

As one of the world's greatest players, Zico inevitably had his fair share of hefty challenges from uncompromising defenders. He was injured in a feisty game with our old rivals Argentina that ended with a sending-off for Maradona, but scored in a 3-1 win.

The 1986 tournament was to prove another disappointment for Brazil and Zico. They went out to France after losing a memorable quarter-final. Zico was carrying an injury and missed a penalty in that game, summing up his unfortunate tag of being unlucky when it came to the World Cup. Even so, that doesn't diminish what a terrific player he was.

10

Celebrating a strike by Serginho, Zico is a picture of joyous goal celebration. Despite the crushing disappointment of going out before the semi-finals, Zico had a great World Cup in 1982. He scored twice against New Zealand, once with a fabulous acrobatic bicycle kick, and scored a marvellous free-kick goal against Scotland.

10

10 Baggio

The Divine No.10

Italian fans have always treated their strikers with passion, veering from reverence to indignation. Few have been so adored as Roberto Baggio. The fact that he played for a large number of club sides may be a factor in his huge popularity, but it was his performances for the *Azzuri*, his colourful character and his special talent that really endeared him to the nation.

Baggio was a mercurial footballer – a great goalscorer and a scorer of great goals. His best was probably in the 1990 group phase game against Czechoslovakia, and it provides a perfect illustration of his many wonderful capabilities. Starting a World Cup game for the first time, all eyes were on him and he didn't disappoint. In the 77th minute he gained possession right on the halfway line beside the left-hand touchline, exchanged passes and glided, as if on a magic carpet, right through the Czech team, sending defenders this way and that, before coolly slipping the ball into the net. It was a fabulous goal, one of the best ever scored by an Italian player, and Baggio had the skills and audacity to pull it off.

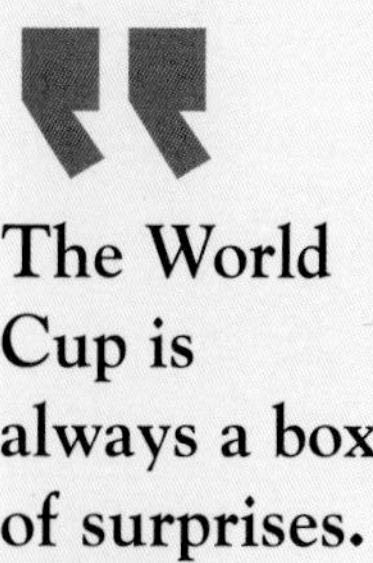

The World Cup is always a box of surprises.

10

◀ Roberto Baggio in action against the Republic of Ireland in the 1990 World Cup quarter-final in Rome. In front of his countrymen, Baggio was only sparingly used, often substituted or introduced as a sub, and only made the No.10 shirt his own in the 1994 tournament.

Baggio wasn't just a flair player. He was competitive, resolute and had the physical and mental toughness all great strikers require. It was part of his make-up that enabled him to score nine goals in 13 World Cup finals matches – an excellent return.

Baggio will for ever be remembered for his miss in the penalty shoot-out of the 1994 World Cup final against my beloved Brazil. Normally so reliable in such situations, Roberto blasted the ball over and Brazil thus secured their fourth World Cup win, but it would be wrong to pin all the blame on Baggio. He wasn't completely fit, and he wasn't the only Italian to miss – both Franco Baresi and Daniele Massaro had already failed to score. But that's what comes with being the No.10: the responsibility weighs heavier, and the public's and media's focus on how you perform is more intense.

There was always more to Baggio than simply being a footballer. In his playing days he was a superstar who valued his privacy but was in demand with the media and autograph hunters alike. In retirement he has put his fame and celebrity to good use, working as a goodwill ambassador for the UN Food and Agriculture Organization and campaigning on hunger issues. In 2004 he auctioned the boots he wore in his last ever game and gave the proceeds to the Organization – a fitting gesture.

10

▶ Baggio samples the unique musical appeal of Scotland on arrival for a game in Glasgow. He was a very modern footballer – cultured, refined, a bit of a philosopher, too. He became a Buddhist, and not out of some passing fancy or fad; he holds his beliefs with sincere conviction. He famously wore a beaded ponytail and after he scored two goals in the 1994 World Cup semi-final win over Bulgaria, the Italian press dubbed him "the divine ponytail". I love that: it reflects the adoration Italians had for the man and also his unique character.

◀
It's worth remembering that Baggio once refused to take a penalty against his beloved Fiorentina while playing for Juventus. I'm not sure that's something I or any other professional could have even contemplated, but it says much about his principled attitude towards the game and life in general.

10 Klinsmann

The Complete Striker

He was once nicknamed the "Golden Bomber" in a nod to his predecessor Gerd Müller, but, to be fair, I believe there was more to Klinsmann's game than that of the original "Bomber". Klinsmann adapted and thrived wherever he played, succeeding in domestic leagues as contrasting as those of Germany, Italy, England and France. Good footballers will invariably do well wherever they play, but Klinsmann had the maturity and dedication to make an emphatic mark anywhere he took to the field of play.

Jürgen Klinsmann was a proven performer virtually throughout his career for both his country and a number of world-renowned clubs. He was a World Cup winner in 1990, victorious in the European Championships in 1996, and won league titles and cups in Germany and Italy. But such statistics do scant justice to his real worth as a striker who had it all.

A No.10 must have good support from his team-mates.

10

◀ Technique in abundance, pace, movement, intelligence, power, courage, strength in the air and on the ground, Klinsmann possessed almost every attribute you could want in a forward. He scored all kinds of goals from all sorts of distances, extracted the best from his team-mates and had the enviable German mentality of never knowing when he was beaten.

10

Despite injury problems that ruled him out of the epic semi-final against England, Klinsmann was a dominating presence in the European Championships of 1996. He scored three goals and led his team to triumph in the final won by an extra time "golden goal" from Oliver Bierhoff. Throughout the tournament, Klinsmann displayed the mixture of hard work, individual excellence and commitment to the team ethic that made him such an outstanding all-round performer.

▶ Klinsmann was an athletic and energetic striker who put himself into situations where he was always at risk from injury – he limped off in the quarter-final against Croatia.

▲
Shaking hands with Her Majesty Queen Elizabeth ahead of the final.

▶
A deserved winner at Euro '96, Klinsmann had inspired his side towards victory and led by example. Such characteristics were to be evident when Jürgen became coach of his country a decade later.

Klinsmann created a real stir in England when he transferred to Tottenham Hotspur in 1994. He arrived with a reputation for being a bit of a diver from his time in Italy and in the World Cup in 1990, and the English fans and media seemed intent on pre-judging and condemning him before he had even kicked a ball. But Jürgen is a smart guy. Not only did he win everyone over with his charm and his performances on the pitch, he made light of his reputation, asking at his first press conference where the nearest diving school was. It was a neat joke and immediately disarmed his critics. He was also clever not to play up to the image of a millionaire superstar, happy to drive around in a humble VW Beetle (though the Ferrari was apparently parked in the garage!). It all worked: within a season he had been named Footballer of the Year by the English press.

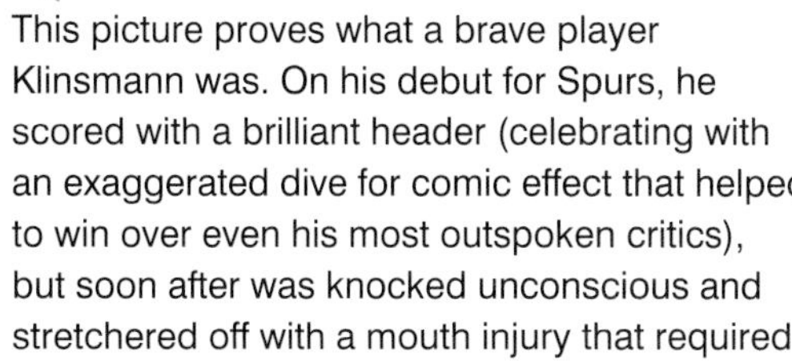

This picture proves what a brave player Klinsmann was. On his debut for Spurs, he scored with a brilliant header (celebrating with an exaggerated dive for comic effect that helped to win over even his most outspoken critics), but soon after was knocked unconscious and stretchered off with a mouth injury that required several stitches.

This is something worth bearing in mind when people complain about strikers feigning injury or seeking to “win” penalties. I was on the receiving end of all the tricks in the defender’s book when I was a player, some of them underhand, others blatantly violent. When you don’t receive the protection you feel you should be getting from referees then sometimes you have to seek an advantage where you can. That’s not to say I condone diving, but, especially in the modern era, when the game is so tactical and defences are so tight, strikers will inevitably look to gain an edge.

It should also be noted that Klinsmann was back playing and scoring again (see overleaf) within four days of this injury. That’s not the behaviour of a cheat, it’s the determination of a courageous man.

Me dive? Never, I always go straight for goal.

Jürgen Klinsmann

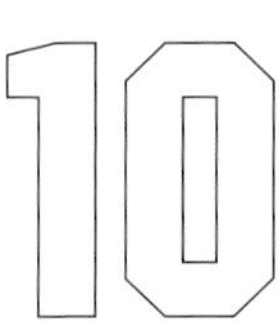

◀
Klinsmann in acrobatic action, scoring with a spectacular scissor-kick volley – almost a bicycle kick, one of my specialities!

Player Profile

CAREER STATS

Jürgen Klinsmann

Name: Jürgen Klinsmann

Born: 1964

International Playing Career: 1987–1998

International Appearances: 108

Goals: 47

Clubs: Stuttgart Kickers, VfB Stuttgart, Internazionale, Monaco, Tottenham Hotspur, Bayern Munich, Sampdoria

Did you know...?

When he was growing up Klinsmann trained to be a baker in his father's shop.

◀ Whenever he returns to the UK, Klinsmann is now a popular visitor.

◀ Klinsmann (left inset) kept playing well into his thirties thanks in part to his dedication to good training and physical preparation.

10

All strikers of course love scoring goals, but few appeared to gain so much joy from the act of putting the ball into the net as Jürgen. He wasn't as prolific as some of his peers (although nearly 285 from 650 games is nothing to complain about) but he took obvious and infectious pleasure in getting on the scoresheet, whether with Germany or in club football.

Klinsmann and team-mates celebrate winning Euro '96.

Klinsmann was tempted back to Germany when he moved to Bayern Munich in 1995, an eventful but successful spell. He won the Bundesliga in 1997 and the UEFA Cup the previous year, scoring against humble Raith Rovers in the process.

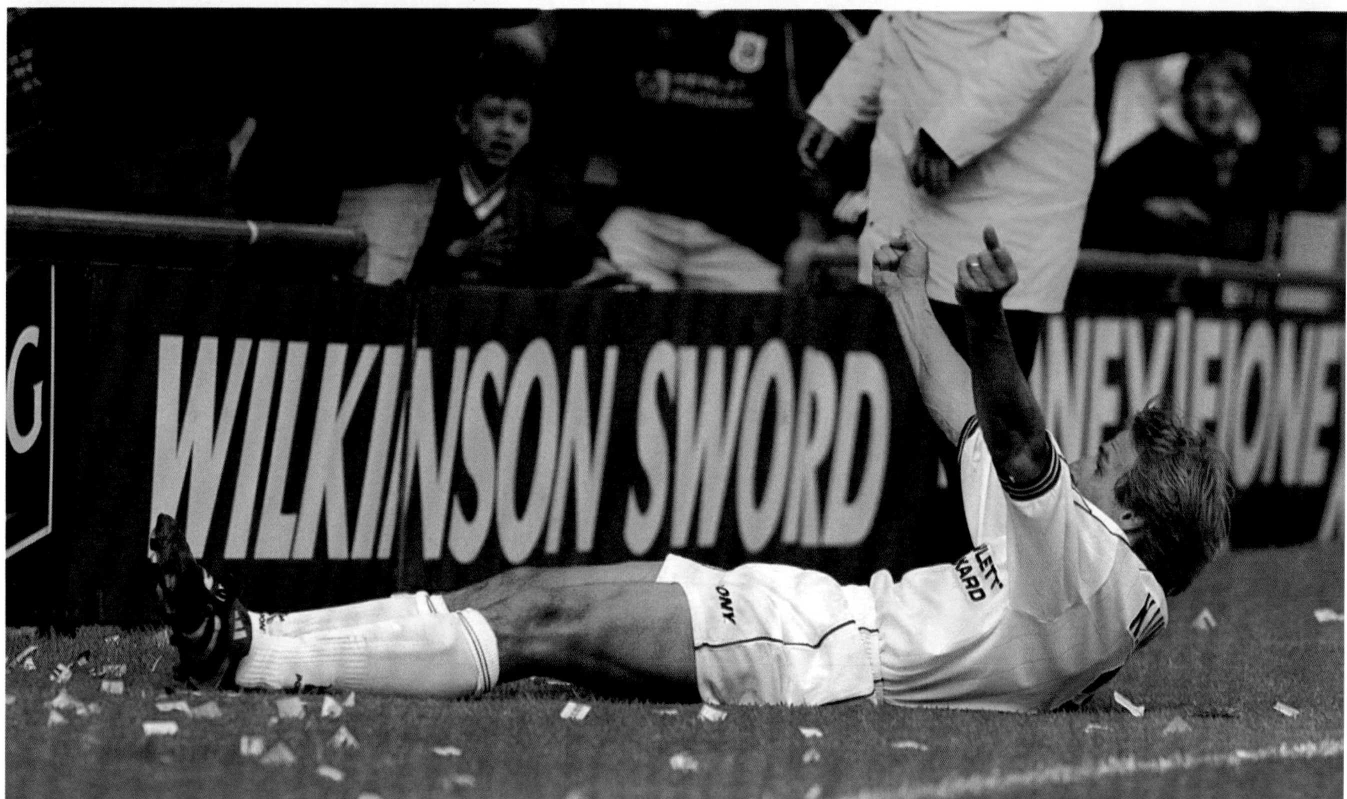

No dive this time – just another happy goalscoring celebration.

10

◀ Jürgen made a dramatic impact as a manager when he took charge of Germany for the 2006 World Cup. Despite his lack of experience he proved to be an inspirational figure who rescued a dispirited German side plagued by infighting and criticism. Against the odds, he took them to the semi-finals. He then spent a disappointing season in charge of Bayern, but I'm sure he'll find a role in which he is again successful. He has a lot more to offer in the future.

10 Milla

Lion of Africa

When I saw Roger Milla at the 1990 World Cup I confess that I had a slight feeling of envy. His birth date had been of some debate, but by common consensus he was 38 when he played for Cameroon in Italia '90. Seeing a guy of such advanced years, pitting himself against the world's best, and captivating the watching billions with his impressive ball-dribbling and goalscoring displays, made me wonder if I'd retired too early.

But Milla was no novelty. He and his Cameroonian team-mates played with an obvious sense of patriotism and purpose, and fully merited their quarter-final placing before finally bowing out with pride intact. We all thought that was the last we would see of Milla but, incredibly, he was back four years later in America, at 42, once again wearing the by now famous green shirt of the "Indomitable Lions".

Excellent player though he was, I don't think anyone is going to pretend Milla is one of the finest strikers in football history. He had a good but unspectacular career playing for a number of French clubs without threatening to break any goalscoring records or capture the sport's biggest prizes. Some readers may wonder why he has been picked when others who have played in the No.10 shirt – the brilliant Michel Platini, is one example that stands out – have not made the selection (though it should be noted that Platini was more of a midfielder than a striker). But in compiling this selection of famous and finest No.10s, Milla deserves inclusion partly because of what he stands for.

I was 17 when I played in the World Cup. But it's the mental age that's key.

10

◀ Milla and Cameroon's achievements were hugely symbolic, because they showed how an African team could compete with and even beat the world's best. Milla was "past it" by the standards of professional football, but his performances heralded a bright future for the game. I am confident that a country from outside the traditional heartlands of Europe and South America will one day win the sport's greatest prize, and players like Milla and teams like Cameroon will have played their part in laying the foundations for making that a reality.

10

Cameroon's progress through Italia '90 was one of those wonderful stories the tournament often manages to provide. They made everyone sit up and notice with a shock defeat of holders Argentina in the opening game. Roger then came on as a sub and scored twice in the next game against Romania and repeated the feat in the next match against Colombia, complete with his trademark celebratory wiggle at the corner. Milla was a clinical finisher and in all he scored five times in 10 World Cup finals matches.

10

10

Cameroon were invited to Wembley to play England in a 1991 friendly in honour of the tremendous battle the Africans gave the English in their Italia '90 quarter-final. Milla was a slightly frozen guest.

◀ Milla waved farewell to football again in 1997 with Indonesian side Putra Samarinda (and trained under Mario Kempes who was working in the country at the time). It had been an eventful 15 years since his World Cup finals debut in 1982, during which time he had been brought out of semi-retirement at the insistence of Cameroon president Paul Biya, and when he became the oldest player to score in the tournament in 1994. Roger now works with the UN as an Aids awareness ambassador. Roger was nicknamed 'Pelé' as a youngster; not a bad name for a striker.

Acknowledgements

Selected sources:

Daily Mirror

FIFA.com

BBC

Rsssf.com

Pelé – The Autobiography (Pocket Books 2007)

Thanks to Adam Powley

All at Mirrorpix, plus Richard Havers, Kevin Gardner, Rebecca Ellis, Elizabeth Stone, Paul Moreton, and all at Haynes and IMG.